The Luftwaffe in the North African Campaign

Werner Held/Ernst Obermaier

THE LUFTWAFFE

A Photo Chronicle

Translated from the German by Don Cox

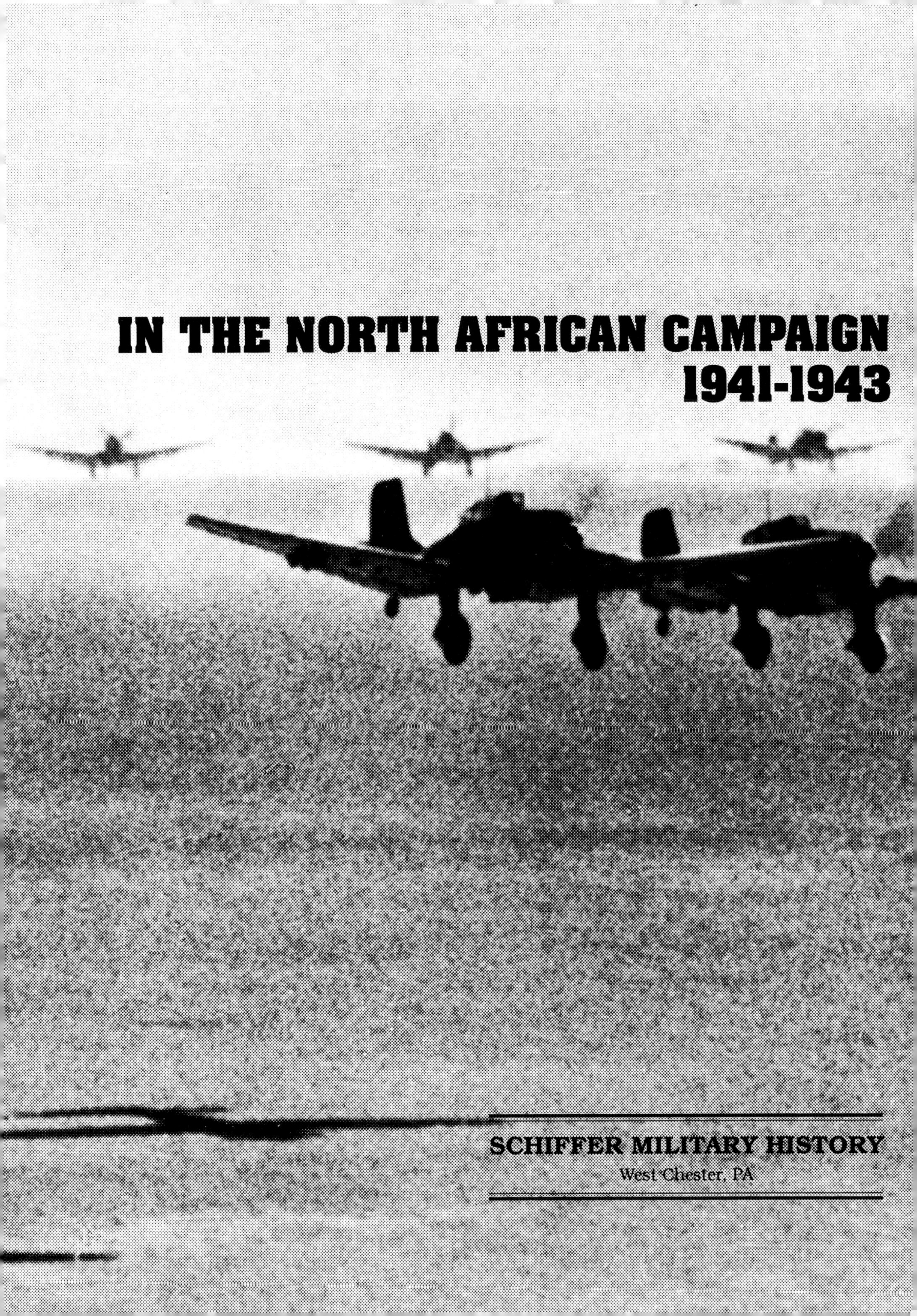

IN THE NORTH AFRICAN CAMPAIGN 1941-1943

SCHIFFER MILITARY HISTORY
West Chester, PA

Dust Jacket Artwork by Steve Ferguson, Colorado Springs, CO.

MUNCHEBERG: MENACE OF MALTA

The Bf 109E-7, "White 12", was the aircraft most often flown by *Oblt.* Joachim Müncheberg, *Staffel-Käpitan* of 7./JG 26, in the 1941 Mediterranean campaign. Müncheberg's "Emil" is camouflaged in standard Luftwaffe day-fighter grays and heavily mottled with RLM 62 green on the fuselage. A white command pennant marks the radio mast and thirty-eight red kill bars are displayed on the yellow rudder, circa late April. All of the JG 26 planes have the yellow nose and tail, red heart and wide white fuselage band. Spinner designs varied.

Müncheberg led the nomadic 7 *Staffel* to Sicily in early April, 1941, and flew combat across the entire span of the Mediterranean theater. In the April-May assault on Malta, Müncheberg held a one-man reign of terror over the RAF Hurricanes. Returning to France two months later, the *Staffel* had acquired 52 theater kills, 25 of which had fallen to the guns of their ace leader whose personal count had climbed to 48.

Müncheberg flew continuous combat on every front for the next two years, recording over 500 missions and 135 victories. Highly decorated and promoted to *Kommodore* of JG 77, he was killed in a clash with U.S. Spitfires over Tunisia on March 23, 1943.

The photographs were provided by: Börngen, Christl, Dreifke, Hauf, Haugk, Helbig, the Kameradschaft of the 9th Staffel III/ZG 26, Maison, Mayer, Muggenthaler H., Muggenthaler M., Oswald, Otte, Pölz, Price, Remmer, Sinner Stahlschmidt, Trenz, Zittier, Zwilling, and the authors.

Translated from the German by Don Cox.

Library of Congress Catalog Number: 91-66336.

Printed in the United States of America.
ISBN: 0-88740-343-3

This title was originally published under the title,
Die Deutsche Luftwaffe im Afrika-Feldzug 1941-1943,
by Motorbuch Verlag, Stuttgart

Published by Schiffer Publishing, Ltd.
1469 Morstein Road
West Chester, Pennsylvania 19380
Please write for a free catalog.
This book may be purchased from the publisher.
Please include $2.00 postage.
Try your bookstore first.

CONTENTS

PREFACE

As a result of various suggestions both from home and abroad, this book uses a mixture of words and photographs in an attempt to provide the interested reader with a greater understanding of German Luftwaffe operations during the African Campaign of 1941-1943.

This book is not intended to be a complete reference work detailing every individual aerial engagement in which the Luftwaffe participated. It was also not within the scope of this pictorial to identify by name or in picture each Luftwaffe unit operating in the African theater or which flew against Malta. Nor is this an aircraft recognition guide, describing an aircraft which operated in North Africa down to its last detail. Nevertheless, we believe that this pictorial, arranged in a chronological fashion, provides a good overview of the Luftwaffe's fight in the struggle for Africa during the years 1941-1943.

The more than 500 carefully selected photographs, which for the most part have never been published before, represent all former members of the Luftwaffe who fought in Africa. They stand for their operations in the Mediterranean and against Malta, for the unforgettable names of Sollum, Bardia, Tobruk, Halfaya Pass, Bir Hacheim, Fort Lamy, the Suez Canal, Alexandria, Alam Halfa, El Alamein and the battles of the "Tunisian Bridgehead."

Each of these names is also a reminder of the Luftwaffe's many missing and fallen soldiers who participated in this theater. And so this book has become a pictorial document for the units of the former German Luftwaffe, for its bomber and dive bomber pilots, the fighter and attack pilots, the reconnaissance and transport crewmen, the air-sea rescue and medevac crews, the paratroopers and the "HG" units, as well as the anti-aircraft crews, all who fulfilled their soldierly duty on the soil of Africa.

Our gratitude goes out to all former members of those Luftwaffe units stationed in Africa who contributed their photos, reports, and suggestions to make this book as accurate as possible. In particular, we owe a special thanks to the following individuals: *Major* a.D. Georg Christl, *Oberst* a.D. Joachim Helbig, Mrs. Margarethe Muggenthaler, *Hauptmann* a.D. Franz Oswald, Mr. Alfred Otte, Kommerzialrat Ing. Hubert Pölz (*Hptmn.* a.D.), Dr. med. Hanna Remmer, Professor Ernst Alexander Zwilling, and Mr. Wolfgang Schilling.

The Authors

The North African Campaign 1941-1943

Benito Mussolini, the fascist dictator of Italy, fancied himself as a latter-day heir of the Caesars. His focus was on the renewal of a great Roman empire extending throughout the Mediterranean and the countries along its shores. Prior to the outbreak of the Second World War his forces were already sitting in Libya. In 1939 he annexed Albania and finally — after initially remaining neutral — entered the war on the side of Germany (only after the quick German victories must have caused him to fear that he was too late for any of the spoils). But the expansive territorial demands which he then brought before Hitler were ignored.

He now saw his opportunity on the soil of Africa. Mussolini therefore gambled on an independent attack against Egypt, which had been occupied by the British since 1882. On 13 September 1940, Italian troops under General Berti crossed the Egyptian border, yet six days later these troops had not advanced beyond the outskirts of Sidi Barani.

Up until 7 December, operations remained confined to local skirmishes. On 7 December 1940, the British, under the command of General Wavell, launched a counterattack and by the 11th of that month the British 7th Armored Division and the 4th Indian had rolled the Italians back across the Libyan-Egyptian border. They pushed relentlessy onward, conquering Bardia, Tobruk, Derna and all of Cyrenaica. When the British forward units finally stopped near el Agheila on 8 February 1941, the only North African colony remaining to Italy was Tripoli.

Mussolini's ambitious plans for victory and glory had turned into a bitter defeat, one which weighed even more heavily as the East African colonies of Eritrea and Ethiopia fell at almost the same time. In a space of ten weeks the British had thrown the Italians back over 1000 kilometers and crushed the 10th Italian Army. They had taken 130,000 prisoners, captured 400 tanks and 845 artillery pieces — and in the process had wiped out ten Italian divisions. The Italian air force, too, was never able to fully recover from the losses it had suffered during these battles.

However, due to the German march into the Balkans, the British were not able to expand upon nor take advantage of their success. Their resources were needed to assist the hard-pressed Greeks. The victorious British troops were therefore pulled out of North Africa and either made ready for operations in Greece or rotated home for rest and relaxation. The British air force also rotated its desert-experienced groups out of the theater.

After the Italian attack had come to a standstill near Sidi Barani on 19 September 1940, the "Duce" immediately turned to Hitler for aid and support. Exactly what form this assistance was supposed to take wasn't entirely clear in the Italian camp. Mussolini wanted tanks; Marshal Badoglio preferred to simply have German Luftwaffe units. When the Italians were forced to retreat before the British counteroffensive Hitler felt obligated to act quickly in support of his Axis partner — who in the meantime had also failed with his campaign in northern Greece. Hitler ordered the organization of a "Sperrverbands Afrika" (lit. an "African Protective Unit"). On 6 February, 1941, The Führer named as its commander a recently promoted *Generalleutnant* who had proven himself exceptionally well as a tank general in the French campaign — *Generalleutnant* Erwin Rommel.

As early as two months prior to this, on 5 December 1940, (which was also before General Wavell's offensive), Hitler had determined that the Luftwaffe was to fly in support of the Italians in the eastern Mediterranean. The X Fliegerkorps under *General der Flieger* Geisler was given this responsibility and deployed to Sicily. This Korps was tasked with the assignment, which it fulfilled to its utmost ability, to carry out, "attacks against British shipping in the straits between Sicily and Tunisia, offensive operations against the island fortress of Malta, support of Italian troops in North Africa, protection of the shipping routes to Libya, strikes against British supply routes in Cyrenaica and in the Suez Canal."

Around noon on 12 February 1941, Rommel arrived at the airfield Castel Benito near Tripoli. The first German soldiers had arrived in Tripoli the day before. These were members of the Berlin-Brandenburgische Aufklärungs-Abteilung 3 (Reconnaissance Battalion 3) under the command of Irnfried Freiherr von Wechmar. The German public first learned of the presence of German soldiers from the reporting office of the Oberkommando of the Wehrmacht (OKW) on 26 February 1941. At the time no one could have guessed that for the next two years the OKW would continue to report on the fighting in North Africa, until on 13 May 1943 it would broadcast the final defeat with the end of the fighting in Tunisia.

On 31 March 1941, Rommel made the first thrusts into Cyrenaica with his newly named "Deutsches Afrikakorps", or DAK. This push quickly grew into a full-blown offensive. On 2 April the city of Agedabia was taken, and on 4 April the German and Italian troops forced their way into Benghazi, where they found great amounts of war material left behind by the vacating British. Rommel didn't stop there, but continued to push further eastwards with two Kampfgruppen. One Gruppe followed the Via Balbia in the direction of Derna, the other targeted the large British staging area and supply base of Mechili. The fort was besieged and fell on 7 April. 2000 men, including four British generals, were taken prisoner. Derna was also taken on the same day.

Ignoring the orders of the OKW and the Italian Comando Supremo, which had only approved further attacks once the 15th Panzer Division arrived in Libya, Rommel pushed further ahead. Tobruk had been turned by the British into a veritable bulwark, yet it was expected to be taken with little effort. However, the attack on 11 April was not successful and the fortress was besieged. One Kampfgruppe struck out in the direction of the Egyptian border, conquering the desert fortress of Bardia on 11 April and Capuzzo on Easter. The Egyptian border was crossed shortly after this, and Sollum and Halfaya Pass were both taken by storm. But then the giant push ground to a halt - on the one hand due to the stiff resistance of the British, and on the other hand due to the massive shortage of supplies, primarily that of fuel for the tanks and vehicles.

Once the DAK had been strengthened, Rommel again attempted to overrun the fortress of Tobruk — which continued to be a thorn in his side. But this time he also utilized the concentrated support of the Luftwaffe. The city put up bitter and fierce resistance, especially by the Australians, and although a rather large break was made in the fortress defenses on 30 April, Tobruk did not fall. Rommel ordered a halt to the German-Italian attacks in the middle of May and continued with the siege, which lasted until 5 December. In the meantime there continued to be much fighting on the Egyptian border with mixed success. On 15-17 June Rommel fought a defensive battle near Sollum, during which the British lost approximately 220 tanks. The British "Operation Battle Axe" had failed and the first large-scale tank battle in the desert was a victory for the Germans thanks to the 88mm Flak guns, which played a primary role in the victory.

In spite of his success, Rommel still had great concerns, primarily because the quantity of supplies reaching his troops left something to be desired. Operating from the island fortress of Malta, the British continually hampered or seriously disrupted the supply lines, especially the sea routes, so that the loss rate of the Axis Powers climbed to 70%. In the long run, these losses were not permissible and led — albeit only beginning in the spring of 1942 — to a large-scale aerial offensive against Malta by the German 2nd Luftflotte and the Regia Aeronautica. This offensive resulted in Malta's airfields and harbor of La Valetta being put out of commission for a time, during which a relatively sufficient amount of supplies made it through to Africa. Nevertheless, the planned conquest of the island by airborne and naval forces was never carried out. This constant threat to the supply lines for Rommel's army and the Italians continued to exist, and in the end was what turned the tide in the North African campaign.

After the failure of "Operation Battle Axe" General Wavell was replaced by General Sir Claude Auchinleck, hitherto the commander in India, who assumed responsibility for the British forces in North Africa on 5 July 1941. On 18 November 1941, the British 8th Army began their offensive and in a series of hard-won battles lasting until January 1942 pushed the German-Italian troops back through Cyrenaica to their initial point of Agedabia. But Rommel didn't give up. In order to preclude any further advance by the enemy, the "Desert Fox", who was thought to have been beaten, struck with his "Panzergruppe Afrika" at the surprised British on 21 January 1942. By 30 January his forces had rolled into Benghazi, the capital of Cyrenaica. In 17 days Rommel and his men succeeded in retaking everything they had been forced to give up over a period of five weeks of heavy fighting and terrible losses. For this outstanding operation Rommel was promoted to *Generaloberst.*

On 26 May 1942, Rommel began his summer offensive. Its primary objective was to initially conquer Tobruk and then continue on in the direction of Egypt, the main target of the entire campaign. The battle raged around the Ain el Gazala position, where several crises had to first be overcome. One of these was when the DAK was in serious danger of being cut off, and was only saved from destruction by a 3 kilometer long front of 88mm Flak guns of the Flak-Regiment 135 under the command of *Oberst* Wolz. But on 10 June the fortress of Bir Hacheim finally fell after a long, hotly contested struggle in which the German Luftwaffe played a particularly important role. With the fall of this fort the way was clear for Rommel and his troops to take Tobruk, which capitulated after a two-day battle on 21 June. 33,000 troops, including the commander of the fortress, General Klopper, were taken prisoner. Rommel was promoted to *Generalfeldmarschall* on the same day.

Rommel wanted to take advantage of this great victory and made the decision to continue his push toward the east. This resulted in a series of "pursuit battles" in Marmarica and western Egypt and the fall of the Mersa Matruh fortress on 29 June 1942. With the troops totally exhausted and the failure of any type of supplies whatsoever to get through, the offensive ground to a mighty halt — 100km short of Alexandria. So close to their prize, the attack had finally stopped in the area of El Alamein. On 30 August, Rommel's units once again took up the attack, but this time failed in their efforts due to the stiff resistance of the British forces. They lost the battle for Alam Halfa, but only after the fuel for the tanks and vehicles ran out and the resupply via the sea and air routes had been completely cut off by enemy forces.

From this point onward Rommel's initiative was lost. It was taken up by the commander — from 12 August — of the British 8th Army, Lieutenant General Bernard Law Montgomery (later promoted to Field Marshal) and his troops.

Malta, in the meantime, had been re-fortified, and even renewed air attacks by the Germans and Italians against the island did not result in a significant improvement in the supply situation. On 23 October, following a massive barrage involving over 900 field and medium guns and uninterrupted attacks by the RAF, the likes of which had not been seen since the First World War, the 8th Army launched its attack against El Alamein. The Axis forces were able to hold fast until the 4 November, but the British finally broke through and the retreat of the German-Italian "Panzerarmee Afrika" was only brought to a halt in February 1943, in Tunisia.

In the interim a second front had developed. In conjunction with the plan of "Operation Torch", 107,000 British and American troops began arriving on 8 November 1942 in Morocco and Algeria under the command of General Eisenhower. They initially struck out eastward, in the direction of Tunisia. The former commanding general of the "Deutsche Afrikakorps", *General der Panzertruppen* Nehring, was entrusted by *Feldmarschall* Kesselring, OB Süd (Oberbefehlshaber Süd, or Commander-in-Chief South), with the task of forming a bridgehead in Tunisia and was given command of all troops who were now enroute by sea and air.

On 10 November 1942, a company of paratroopers under the command of Hauptmann Sauer landed in Tunisia, which gradually assumed control of the city and harbor of Tunis. More importantly, they were able to secure both of the airfields of Tunis for the arriving paratroopers and army units. *General* Nehring concentrated all units which had landed, occupied the cities of Gabes, Sousse, and Sfax, and erected a front line stretching over 500 kilometers.

Reinforced by the newly arrived 10th Panzerdivision, the Italian "Superga" division, and the heavy Panzer ("Tiger") Abteilung 501, the soldiers under *General* Nehring won the Battle of Tebourba. The American 1st U.S. Armored Division and the 11th British Brigade suffered serious casualties in this battle; 134 combat vehicles were destroyed and 1100 prisoners were taken. The excellent performance of the 20th Flak-Division under *Generalmajor* Neuffer, with its 88mm Flak guns, played a decisive role in defeating the enemy tanks.

The second phase of the fight for the Tunisian Bridgehead began on the 10th of December with the battle of Medjez el Bab and continued, with mixed success on both sides, until the middle of February. From 14-17 February 1942 *Generaloberst* von Arnim led his 5th Panzerarmee in Operation "Frühlingswind" against the Allies in an attempt to break the back of the enemy units at Faid Pass. At Sbeitla, the U.S. 1st Armored Division lost over 100 tanks and 2000 of its soldiers were taken prisoner. In spite of this, a constant rain of bombs from Allied aircraft forced von Arnim to break off the attack on the morning of the 17th, especially since any further attempt to advance against the numerically and logistically superior Allied forces was hopeless.

Even *Generalfeldmarschall* Rommel, despite the outstanding exhibition of bravery on the part of his troops and his own leadership abilities, was not able to take Tebessa by storm with his "Panzerarmee Afrika" on 17-22 February 1942, and thereby complete the hoped-for encirclement of the enemy. On 6 March he flew to the Führer's headquarters with the intent of getting Hitler's approval for a massive operation to rescue the soldiers fighting in Tunisia. Hitler categorically refused any such operation and at the same time forbad Rommel to return to Africa. With this action, the "Desert Fox" was forced to leave the theater after two years of fighting, during which he had achieved truly great victories, victories which he was only forced to concede in the face of the logistical superiority of the enemy and the misconceptions of the German leadership (which viewed the war in North Africa as nothing more than a "sideshow").

The end in Tunisia now came very quickly. After the British 8th Army broke through the Mareth Line at the beginning of April, they joined up with the 1st Army on 7 April. Two weeks later, on 22 April, the Allies' final offensive began, which in spite of the brave resistance put up by the Axis troops ended in the total capitulation of all German-Italian units on 13 May. Only a few hundred soldiers managed to escape to Sicily. 130,000 Germans and 180,000 Italians were taken as prisoners of war. 18,594 Germans and 13,748 Italians remained behind, buried on African soil. In addition there were over 3400 German and 8821 Italian soldiers missing in action. The number of soldiers who lost their lives while crossing the Mediterranean by plane and ship has not been determined even today. When the final figures are in, the number of fallen soldiers in this totally senseless war reaches to over 100,000.

Among the dead and missing in action are members of the Luftwaffe units who perished in the struggle for the Black Continent and the Mediterranean. In the truest sense of camaraderie, they supported the Heer and Kriegsmarine to the best of their ability. Not only did the flak gunners, paratroopers, pilots and crew of the flying units display almost incredible performance, but this was also exhibited by the trusty "blackmen", the ground crew of the weapons and aircraft. Whether under enemy attack or in the burning heat — when temperatures often climbed to over 120 degrees — they stuck to their difficult tasks. No OKW office ever reported on their efforts. But in the minds of the pilots and crew they remain unforgettable, for it was only through the efforts of these men that they were victorious, and many owed their lives to the "blackmen."

The III/ZG 26 arrives in Treviso in Southern Italy. After the ground personnel arrived the unit moved to Palermo.

Left page: **The Staffeln were equipped with drop tanks for the long flight across the Mediterranean Sea.**

17 January 1941: II Gruppe of KG 26 "Löwen-geschwader" flew operations against Malta from its base in Sicily.

Left page:
Ju 87s of II/StG 2 and I/StG 1 targeted British ship convoys, where they enjoyed considerable success.

The 4th Staffel of the (Kampf-) Lehrgeschwader 1 seen approaching Malta. Under the fuselage of each aircraft are two 1000kg bombs and a 500kg bomb.

The III/ZG 26 flew surveillance missions and anti-shipping strikes from Trapani (Sicily).

After a mission this plane nosed over. Cause: defective tires.

◄ A deadly cargo! Wing-mounted bombs on a Ju 88.

Ju 88s of the ▲ KüFlGr 806 in operations against Malta.▼

The 900 liter capacity plywood drop tanks seen here being refuelled.

Right page:
The 7/ZG 26 forms up over Sicily and flies across the Mediterranean to Africa, where they're met by Italian Askaris.

German and Italian merchant vessels and warships, as well as flying boats from the combined air forces, seen here in Tripoli's harbor. For many months this was the most important supply harbor for the Deutsche Afrika-Korps.

Right page: Heavy equipment is used to unload heavy goods.

623

First contact is made with the locals in the new surroundings, and snapshots are taken for the family albums.

"Zerstörer" Over Africa

The history of the operations of the German "Zerstörer" (Destroyer) over Africa is closely interwoven with the operational history of a Gruppe — the famous III/ZG 26.

Following the costly Battle of Britain and the subsequent rearmament, this Gruppe moved in December 1940 and January 1941 and became the first unit of the German Luftwaffe in the Mediterranean area, only leaving the theater after two and a half years of operations. It had served the longest in this combat arena, enjoying great success as well as suffering heavy losses — and in doing so made a name for itself in the annals of the German Luftwaffe.

The primary mission of the Gruppe was and remained the protection of the air and sea routes from Sicily to Tripoli as well as the interception of enemy shipping. In addition, it was also tasked with reconnaissance missions and "freie Jagd", or fighter sweeps. After the landing of the Deutsche Afrika-Korps there came the important task of attacking ground targets of all types. For example, in a matter of a few days in February 1941 the Gruppe succeeded in totally annihilating the British vanguard in the area of Agheila-Agedabia. Not only that, but it was also able to deal a serious blow to the enemy's main columns and supply routes, to halt the enemy's advances, and to provide constant support to Rommel's first offensive which followed.

The operations and locations changed with the advances and retreats of the Afrika-Korps. But throughout the campaign the first and greatest priority was given to the protection of the supply routes. As a rule, one Staffel was based in Africa while the remainder of the Gruppe flew from Sicily and Crete. During critical operations the entire Gruppe would be concentrated in Africa. It was natural that the Zerstörer would be a participant in the suppression of Malta; these aircraft also carried out an exceptionally high number of low-level attacks during the battle for Tobruk. Another Staffel, the newly-formed 10/ZG 26 flying the Ju 88, joined the Gruppe at the beginning of April 1942. Again and again the Zerstörer pilots proved themselves exceptionally well in this theater of war, in spite of their small numbers and the enormous difficulties which they faced. It is therefore not surprising to note that five members of III/ZG 26 were awarded the Knight's Cross to the Iron Cross for their service in Africa.

With the exception of III/ZG 26 other Zerstörer units were only stationed in the combat zone for brief periods of time. One of these was the III/ZG 26 which was equipped with the Messerschmitt's Bf 109 and Me 210 and primarily flew fighter-bomber missions. Messerschmitt Bf 110 aircraft were also operated by other Luftwaffe units, especially in the tactical reconnaissance and night fighter roles, and there they also fulfilled their often difficult and diverse tasking. The battles in Tunisia once again required the Zerstörer aircraft to fly the tough and dangerous missions of fighter escort for the air and sea transport routes, as well as to conduct low-level attacks along the new front. After Tunisia was lost, the Zerstörers were transferred either to central Italy or, in some cases, back to the Reich itself. Thus concluded a fateful chapter in the rich and colorful history of this weapon.

Protecting African airspace with Bf 110s and Italian Fiat Cr 42 fighters.

Left page:
Flying escort for ships and Ju 52s.

Supplies for Rommel. These supplies include this Fiesler Fi 156 "Storch" (Stork), the most famous all-purpose, liason and observation aircraft of the Luftwaffe.

Ground crewmen at work. Since the units have not yet received their full complement of personnel, natives are used as substitutes and assistants.

Right page:
28 March 1941 at the Gela airfield in Sicily: *Oberleutnant* Müncheberg, Staffelkapitän of the 7/JG 26, returns from his 200th combat mission, during which he scored his 33rd kill.

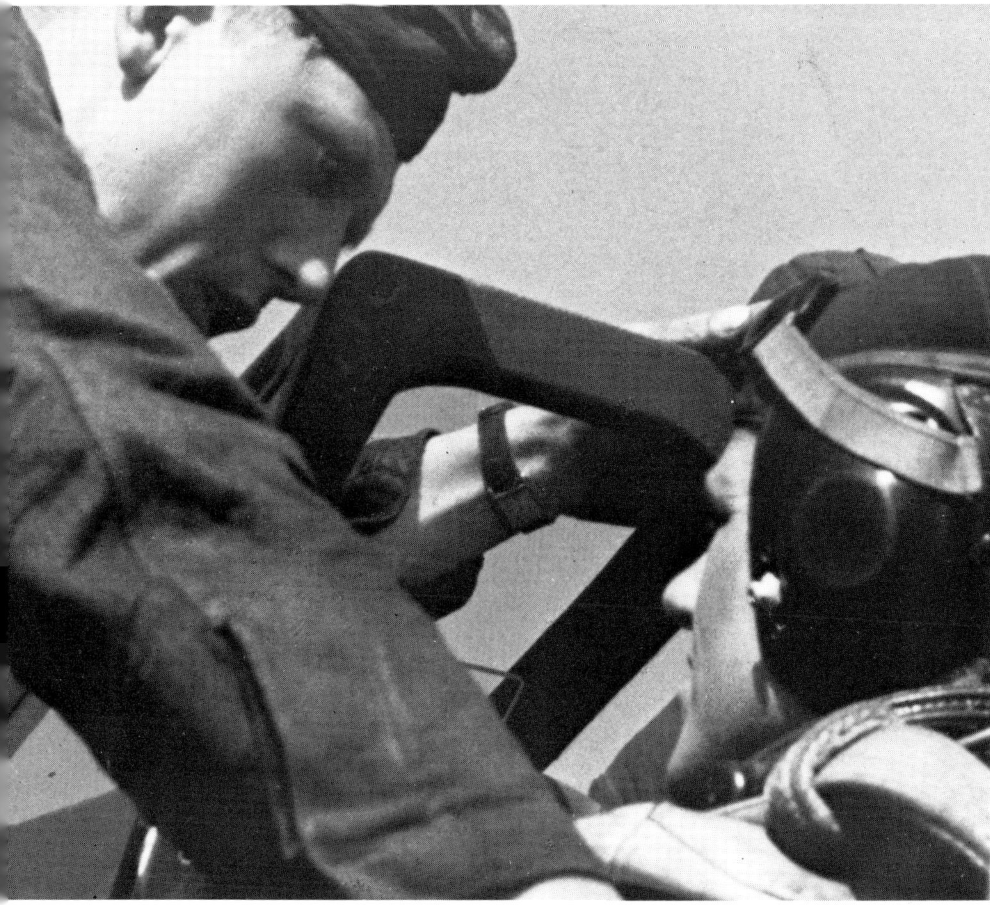

A British fleet is sighted on 29 March and immediately attacked by Stukas. They concentrated their attack on the biggest target, an aircraft carrier.

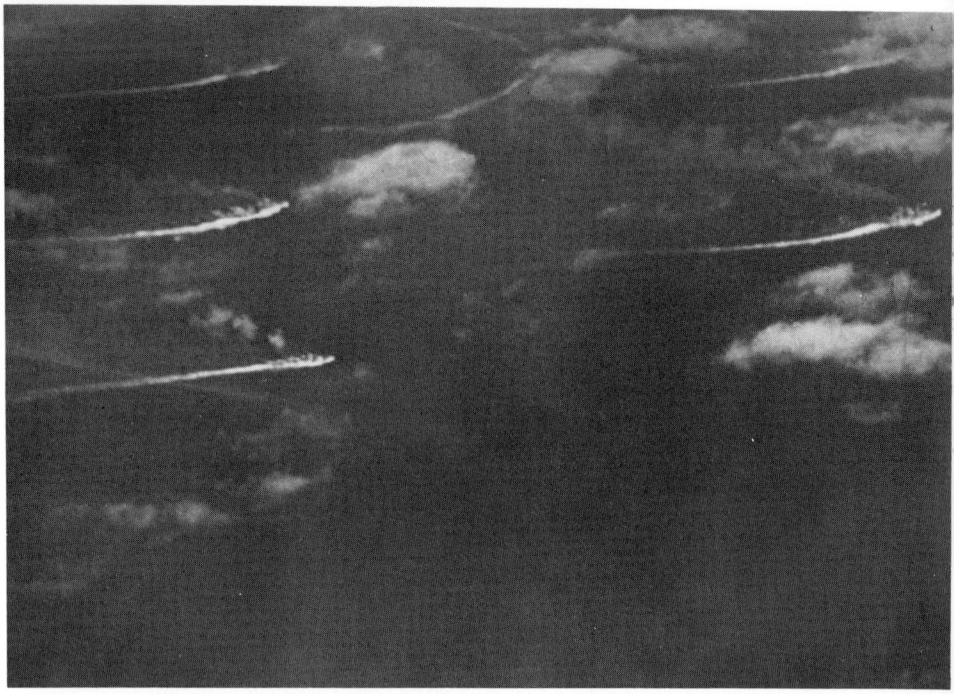

Right page:
Italian Fiat G-50 fighters in flight over the harbor and city of Tripoli, where they provide cover for the ships and the valuable cargo being offloaded.

813
813

Hauptmann Christl — Kapitän of the 7th Staffel of ZG 26 — checks out the Gruppo insignia of his Italian fighter pilot comrades.

German Ju 52 transports are also used to carry Italian troops to Africa.

The view from an escorting Bf 110 showing the group of Ju 52 transports in flight over the Med.

The view from the transport gunner's position looking out over the other transports.

The pilots of 7/ZG 26 have safely brought their charges to their destination. The Staffelkapitän, *Hptm.* Christl, is conducting the debriefing.

◀ The German-Italian counteroffensive in Libya began on 24 March 1941. An endless stream of tanks and vehicles passed eastward through this Italian victory memorial, the Arco di Fileni on the border between Tripolitania and the Cyrenaica. For many men this was a path leading in one direction only.

The 1st Staffel of JG 27 was the first German fighter unit to land in North Africa, beginning combat operations from the Ain el Gazala airfield on 19 April 1941. Soon the Gruppe's emblem, a native African and lion's head, became known among both friend and foe alike.

The pilots of I/JG 27 quickly adapt themselves to the strange conditions of the African theater and score their first victories. The lower picture shows a destroyed Hurricane of an unknown squadron with the name "Kiwi" below the cockpit.

Staffel tents of 6/StG 2 on the edge of the airfield in Derna.

The commanding general of X Fliegerkorps, *General der Flieger* Geisler, greets the victorious pilots of 3/StG 3 in Sicily (from left to right): *Oblt.* Riedinger, *Oblt.* Warncke, *Lt.* Stry. All three fell to the enemy.

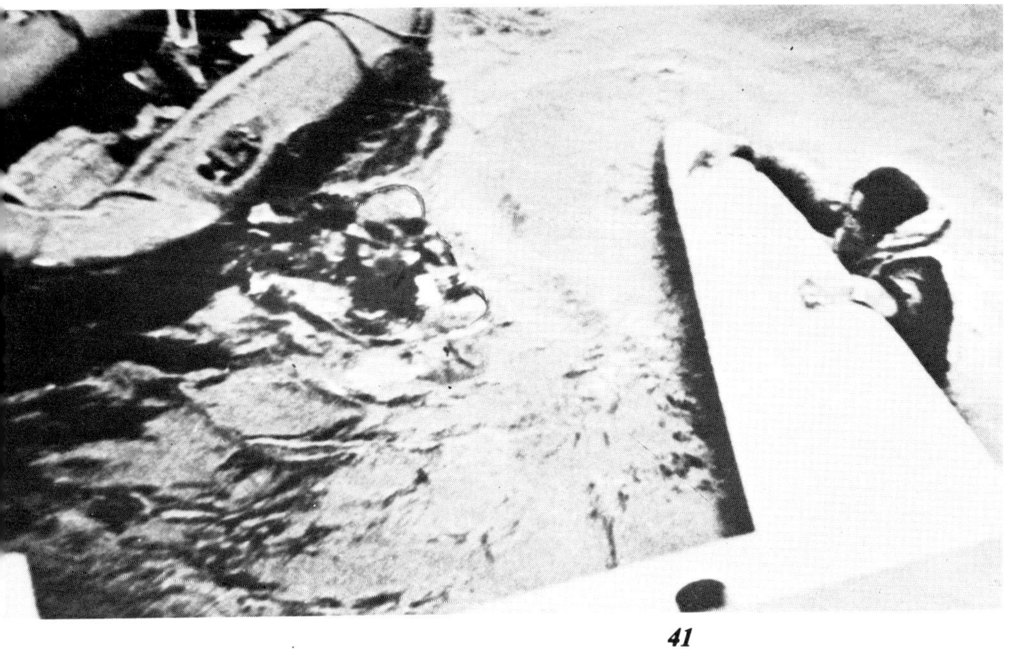

Lady Luck smiles once again! *Lt.* "Theo" Nordmann (next to the raft) and his radioman *Uffz.* Rothe of 8/StG 1 were forced to ditch in the Mediterranean due to engine damage. After 28 hours they were finally rescued by an Italian rescue seaplane.

The Fi 156 "Storch" and the "Tante Ju" are joyfully welcomed and eagerly awaited, the "Storch" because it's carrying a missing comrade back from the desert and the Ju 52 because it has desperately needed fuel on board.

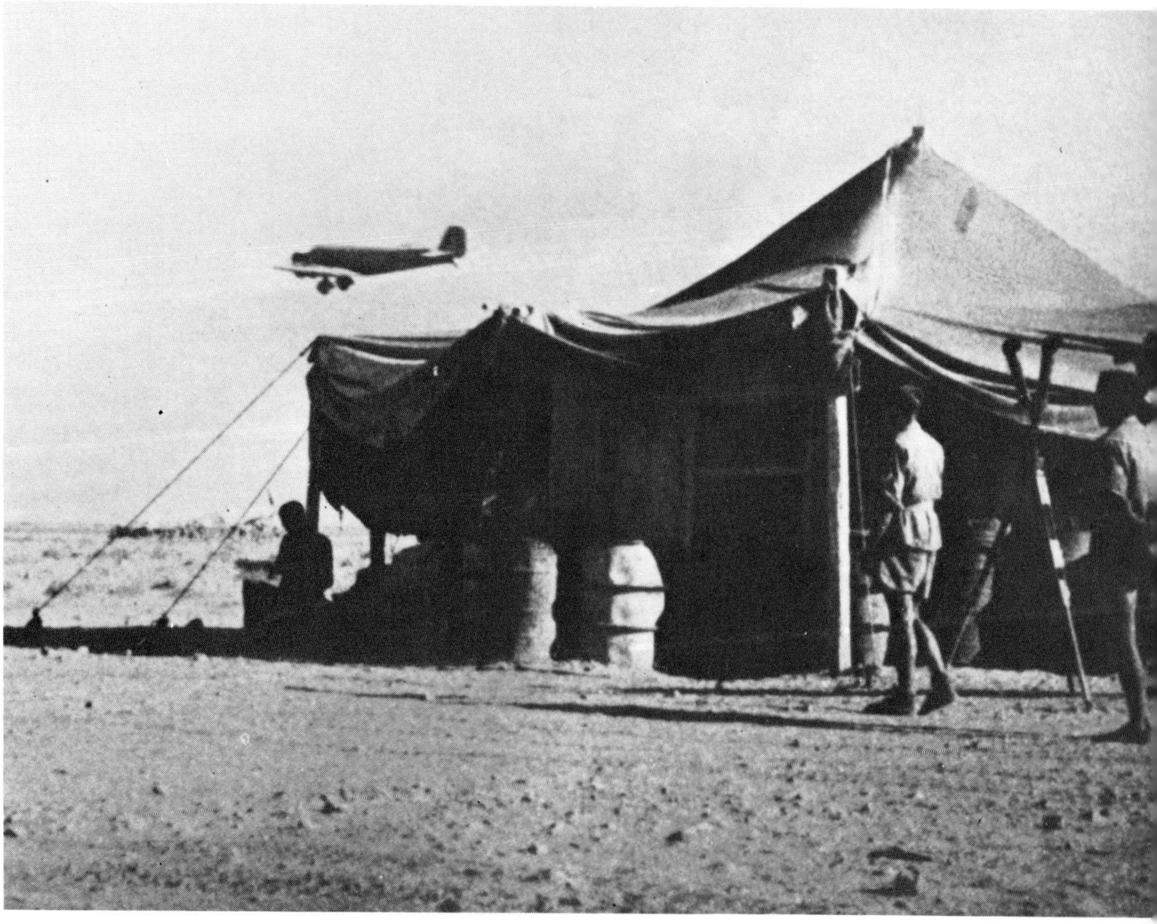

FIGHTERS OVER THE DESERT

On 19 February 1941, 13 Ju 52 transports took off from Döberitz near Berlin and headed south. On board these aircraft were the technical and intelligence personnel of I/JG 27, under the leadership of *Oblt.* Heydecke. Following stopovers in Treviso and Comiso they landed at the airfield of Castel Benito in Tripoli on 27 February. In so doing, they became the first members of a German fighter Geschwader to set down in North Africa. Following a brief stint in the Balkans, the Gruppe's pilots gathered together in Munich in April 1941, where their Bf 109 aircraft were being modified for operations in Africa.

As the first flying unit of JG 27, the 1st Staffel under *Oblt.* Redlich landed in Ain el Gazala on 18 April 1941. They began combat operations as early as the next day, and by and by the other Staffeln and the headquarters unit joined them at their airfield on the Bomba Bay. This location was home to the men of JG 27 for more than seven months. Until September 1941 1/JG 27, under the command of "Edu" Neumann (from 8 July 1942 the Kommodore of the entire Geschwader) alone bore the brunt of fighter combat over the desert. Only in June and July of 1941 were they given support, by *Hptm.* Joachim Müncheberg's 7/JG 26 (see dust jacket). In September 1941 II Gruppe joined battle, and when the headquarters unit and III Gruppe arrived in Africa in December, the entire Geschwader was operating together for the first time since the Battle of Britain in the previous year. North Africa remained the operations area for JG 27 up until the end of 1942; following a brief period of rest in Sicily, II Gruppe also took part in the battle for Tunisia.

For twenty long months JG 27 operated in Africa, and was considered simply as the German "Afrika-Jagdgeschwader." The Geschwader had 1300 confirmed kills to its credit, including over 700 Curtiss fighters, over 300 Hurricanes and more than 100 Spitfires. Under the outstanding leadership of *Major* Woldenga and *Oberstlt.* Neumann, many pilots contributed to the notable success of the Geschwader. The names of Bendert, Franzisket, Homuth, Körner, Marseille, Rödel, Schroer, Schulz, Sinner, Stahlschmidt and Steinhausen represent all of their other fellow pilots of JG 27. The ground personnel, too, played a major role in the success of the pilots, for without their almost superhuman efforts in this theater the victories would not have been possible.

As mentioned earlier, 7/JG 26 "Schlageter" was another participant in the struggle for North Africa in the months of June and July of 1941. III/JG 53 "Pik As" also participated in the campaign in December 1941 and again from May to October 1942. In addition, 6/JG 3 "Udet" (in April 1942) and 4/JG 53 "Pik As" (from September 1942) were also deployed to Africa. From November of 1942 JG 77, with its headquarters unit and all three Gruppen, was also engaged in the fighting in North Africa and Tunisia. From El Alamein to Tunis, JG 77 followed the retreat of the army across Africa. Under the leadership of *Major* Müncheberg (killed on 23 March 1943 in Tunisia) and *Major* Steinhoff, the Geschwader earned many a hard-won victory in operations against the superior Allied air forces. JG 53 "Pik As", commanded by *Oberstleutnant* Freiherr von Maltzahn, fought bitterly and successfully in Tunisia, where it had landed as the first German fighter unit in November of 1942. As they flew to Sicily from Korbous (on Tunisia's Cap Bon peninsula) at the beginning of May 1943 the men of this Geschwader were also the last pilots to leave the theater, some squeezing as many as three ground crewmen into one Bf 109. From November 1942 II Gruppe of JG 51 "Mölders" was likewise based in the Mediterranean and operated in Tunisia. During the same month, II/JG 2 "Richthofen" was also transferred to Sicily from the Channel and flew operations over Tunisia with their Focke-Wulf Fw 190 aircraft until the end of March 1943.

Although for the most part they found themselves fighting a lost cause, the fighter pilots were able to achieve considerable victories, but in doing so also absorbed punishing losses in both pilots and ground personnel. Since there are no exact figures for all German fighter units in this combat theater, it can be assumed that the following data is representative of all fighter pilots in Africa.

The 1300 confirmed aerial victories of JG 27 can be compared to the approximately 200 Messerschmitt fighters lost by the unit in air combat (this figure does not include the large number destroyed on the ground). 37 pilots were killed, among them the "virtuoso of the German fighter aces", Hans-Joachim Marseille; 29 were missing-in-action, and 27 were taken prisoners-of-war.

Right page:
Along with hours of happiness there were also times of tragedy. The upper photo shows the remains of *Uffz.* Hans Sippel's Bf 109 from I/JG 27. Sippel, who was credited with four kills, fell on 21 April 1941 in a dogfight with British fighters near Tobruk. One day later *Ofhr.* Pomsch, also from the same unit, was critically wounded in a dogfight and died the following day. They were laid to rest in the "Weisses Haus" (White House) cemetery west of Tobruk.

1./A.R.75
gef. 21. 4. 41
Oberfähnrich und
Heinz
Flugzeugführer
Pompsch
geb. 3.10.19
gef. 23.4.41
I./JG.27

At the edge of the airfield: army comrades watch a Bf 110 on final approach.

At the edge of the city of Syrte. A Bf 109E of I/JG 27 is refueled and readied for another sortie by the ground crew.

A tranquil picture in the middle of war! An oasis between Tripoli and Zabratta.

The battle for Malta continues. Pilots of 7/JG 26 studying a map prior to their mission.

Oblt. Müncheberg, Staffelkapitän of 7/JG 26 "Schlageter." In the spring of 1941 he succeeded in shooting down 14 Hurricanes over Malta, making him the most successful fighter pilot in the region (see dust jacket).

On 4 May 1941, the massive 10000 ton Italian freighter "Birmania" exploded while its cargo of ammunition was being unloaded. The Italian auxiliary cruiser "Citta di Bari", resting nearby and loaded with fuel, was also blown sky-high. The cause of this disaster were 10kg German aerial bombs, which became armed during unloading due to poorly assembled packing crates.

Ju 87 B-2s of II/StG 2 approaching Tobruk. The Stukas played a major role in the victories in Africa, but at a high cost to themselves.

The aircraft and weapons are overhauled during the brief rest periods, and after the work is done there's still time to enjoy some well earned fruits.

The Staffel insignia of the highly distinguished 7/ZG 26.

One of 7/ZG 26's kills following a British attack on the Derna airfield.

Yet another familiar Staffel emblem: the rooster of 9/ZG 26.

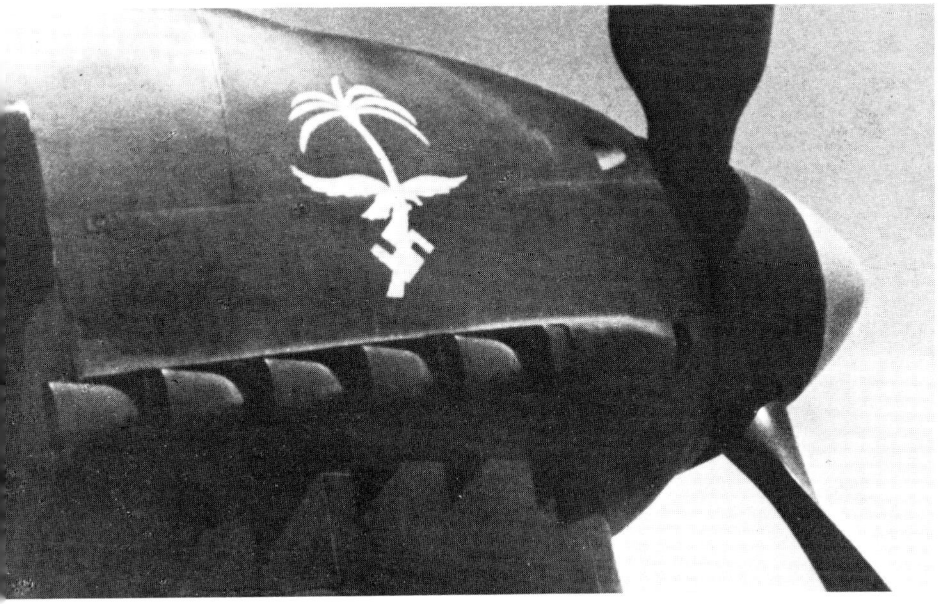

Even the Stukas had their emblems! One of the best known was the "African Palm", which was carried on the right side of the engine cowling by those units of StG 2 which flew in Africa.

One of the most spectacular undertakings of the Luftwaffe took place on 17 January 1941, prior to the arrival of the Afrika Korps. It was carried out by *Major* I.G. Harlinghausen, Chief of Staff of the X Fliegerkorps, seen here with Wearer of the Knight's Cross *Hptm.* Wieting. With eight He 111s of II/KG 26 he took off from Benghazi to attack a convoy reported in the Suez Canal, a one-way distance of 1100km. A severe storm prevented all but one of the aircraft from returning to base. All the remaining aircraft ran out of fuel and were forced to make emergency landings in the desert. Three crews were made prisoners-of-war; Harlinghausen and his men were found by *Oblt.* Kaupisch after four days and rescued from the desert by an He 111.

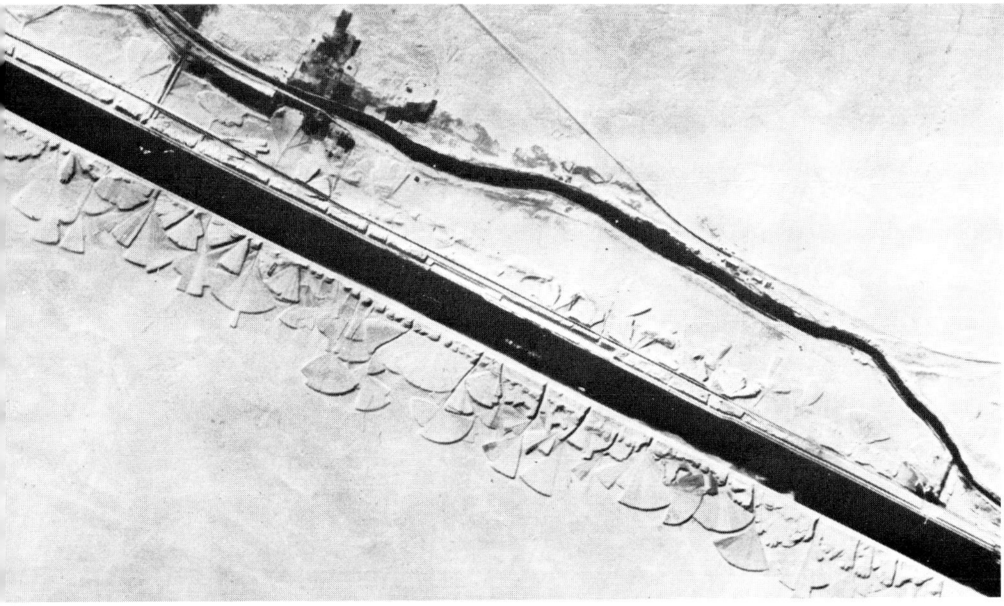

Two photographs taken by a long-range reconnaissance aircraft on 23 May 1941. The above photo shows the Suez Canal approximately 20km north of the city of Suez. A destroyed freighter can be seen in the upper left. The photo below shows a British troop encampment on the Canal near El Qantara.

Reconnaissance played a critical role for both sides. The results quite often made a difference between victory and defeat during the various operations and battles. The photos show British and German recon units in operation.

Left page:
Stuka Ju 87s and the Ju 88 (which was also capable of dive bombing) bore the brunt of attacks on shipping targets, where they enjoyed considerable success. In addition, the courageous torpedo bomber units of the Regia Aeronautica also displayed great effectiveness in the anti-shipping role. The bottom photo shows SM 79 torpedo bombers.

Last minute preparations are made prior to takeoff. While the munitions crewman feeds the ammo belts into the aircraft's onboard guns and the bombs are mounted, the crew wait in front of their Ju 87 (parked in a temporary revetment) and concentrate on the difficult mission ahead of them.

Right page:
The aircraft of II/StG 2 calmly assume attack formation, then dive in a right echelon formation on the target.

T6
M

Lt. Werner Schroer of JG 27 on a visit with his Italian comrades. One and a half years later found him the most successful fighter pilot in Africa next to Marseille, with 61 kills to his credit.

Hptm. Gerhard Homuth, Kapitän of 3/JG 27, later commander of I/JG 27, was also one of the great aces in North Africa. He managed to score 46 victories in this theater. However, fate caught up with him in Russia after nearly 450 combat missions and a total of 63 kills. On 2 August 1943 he failed to return from a combat mission to Orel and was declared missing in action.

Left page:
The bombs are on the target! The Stukas pull up under heavy fire from British anti-aircraft guns and fly back to their home airfield under the protection of Italian fighters.

View of a fighter airfield in the desert. This is what nearly every airfield looked like.

These Ju 52s have nearly reached their destination, the airfield at Derna. They and their valuable cargo are eagerly awaited by the troops there.

Those on leave were also aboard and now, heavily laden, make their way back to their units.

The command post for the transport pilots is seen here at the airfield in Derna.

A Bf 109 E/Trop of I/JG 27 shortly before lifting off.

A view into the trailer of *Hptm.* "Edu" Neumann, the commander of I/JG 27. The interior walls of this former circus wagon, which had already "seen action" in France, were decorated with a painted frieze. Each pilot in the Gruppe was represented as a native, and with every kill a palm frond was added to that pilot's skirt. In the center is the insignia of the Gruppe, a native's and a lion's head, which was recognized throughout the entire *Afrika Korps.* The Gruppe, however, had this emblem long before it came to Africa since its former commander, *Hptm.* Riegel, was an enthusiastic supporter of the colonial movement.

The Gruppen-Adjutant of I/JG 27 flies escort for the Stukas.

"Flak nach vorn!"

"Get the AA guns up front!" — This order was heard again and again in crisis situations on the battlefields of WWII, and the African theater was no exception. The Luftwaffe's anti-aircraft units stationed there played a double role — defense against enemy aircraft and engagement of ground targets. They fulfilled both of these roles brilliantly, especially in operations on the front line in close support of tank units. Their most powerful weapon, the 88mm anti-aircraft gun, became a nightmare for the enemy in Africa. These guns almost never failed when utilized against bunkers and tanks, as well as numerous other ground targets.

The first AA units landed in Africa in March of 1941 in conjunction with the 5th Leichte (Light) Division (later the 21st Panzer Division). They were the I/33 (mot.trop.) under Hptm. Fromm, shortly followed by the Stab (HQ)/Flak-Rgt. 102. Both units were equipped with a mixed AA battalion and a light AA battalion. These units participated in the first successful advance by Rommel and performed admirably in several of the battles, including the Battle of Halfaya Pass at the end of May 1941. In cooperation with the tanks they played a decisive role in the summer Battle of Sollum from 15-18 June 1941, where the I/33 and the I/18 once again distinguished themselves. Flak guns and tanks accounted for the loss of approximately 220 British tanks and won the first large-scale tank battle fought in the desert.

The AA units in Africa continued to prove themselves effective weapons as the struggle continued, whether in a ground battle used in a defensive or offensive role, or in the rear areas, protecting the harbors and airfields so vital for troop supplies. They fought at Bardia, El Gazala, Bir Hacheim and Tobruk, just to name a few of the hotly contested sites. The 88mm batteries of Flak Regiment 135 successfully fended off a particularly threatening attack of the British 7th Armored Division in the area of El Adem on 12 July 1942, and on 27 July Oberst Wolz saved the day with four heavy AA batteries (88mm guns, primarily from Flak Rgt.135) positioned along a 3km long "flak front."

The AA units also took part in the fighting around the Alamein position and the costly retreat which followed. On 14 December 1942, the batteries of I/46 under *Major* Wegener experienced a rather unusual victory. In an artillery duel with four British destroyers they succeeded in knocking the "Zulu" and the "Sikh" (each of 2400t displacement) out of commission.

A second front was formed in Tunisia beginning on 7/8 November. The flak gunners, primarily those of the 19th and 20th Flak Divisions, fought bravely to the bitter end in the so-called "Tunisian Bridgehead." The Flakkampfgruppe of *Oberst* Wolz, deployed in support of German tank advances and as "firemen" in shoring up defenses, repeatedly distinguished themselves in combat (e.g. on 27 March 1943 at the battle of El Hamma by destroying 30 American tanks). The remnants of the 19th and 20th Flak Divisions, having been bled dry from incessant fighting, were forced to capitulate in May 1943.

The flak gunners of the Luftwaffe gave a commendable accounting of themselves in the more than two years of fighting. 16 of them, including two *Gefreiter,* were awarded the Knight's Cross to the Iron Cross. In spite of constant difficulties of all kinds with supplies and the material superiority of the Allied forces on both land and in the air, the AA artillery gave its best in all situations in the African Campaign and fulfilled its soldierly duty to the utmost from the first to last day of operations. Their sacrifice and efforts remain unforgotten in the history of the German Luftwaffe.

A busy day at an airfield occupied by a variety of German and Italian aircraft.

Protected by Italian Fiat fighters, Ju 87 Stukas fly successful missions against British merchant ships off the North African coast.

Operations of the 88mm flak guns of the I/FlaRgt 33 (mot) during the summer battle of Sollum from 15-17 June 1941. The British were not successful in their attempt to take the Halfaya position and move on past Hill 208. Flak guns and friendly tanks destroyed more than 220 enemy tanks and won the largest desert tank battle up to that time. For their action during this battle *Oblt.* Schwabach, *Hptm.* Fromm and *Wachtmeister* Melzer (opposite, center photo, from left to right) were awarded the Knight's Cross. The graves of their unforgotten comrades were left behind.

† 16.6.1941
Curt Perschmann
† 16.6.41

Rommel and Kesselring kept in close contact with each other. This Focke-Wulf Fw 58 C "Weihe" was used as a liaison aircraft and was popular with Rommel.

Feldmarschall Kesselring seen putting on a parachute before boarding a Ju 87 and flying on to his next operations briefing.

A view of the airfield at Derna, one of the most well-known fields in all of North Africa.

The edge of the airfield is littered with the burnt-out wrecks of the British. The picture above shows a Hurricane and below can be seen a Westland Lysander.

A Ju 87 of StG 3 is ready for takeoff at a forward airfield in the desert.

Oberstlt. Walter Sigel, one of the best-known leaders in the Stuka forces. He participated in the entire North African campaign and from April 1942 to April 1943 was commander of StG 3. On 2 September 1942 he was awarded the Oak Leaves to the Knights Cross for both his individual performance as well as the actions of his men. On 8 May 1944 he too met a pilot's death when his Fiesler "Storch" crashed in the Trondheim Fjord during an inspection flight.

This is what the results of a British fighter-bomber attack on the airfield looked like. The burnt-out remains of a Ju 87 are being examined.

Left page: **But the enemy did not always enjoy such victories. This crew of a 20mm flak gun in the parking area of III/ZG 26 managed to shoot down one of the attackers. The crew was buried next to the remnants of their Blenheim.**

Evening settles in on the desert, betraying an almost happy and peaceful world. Unfortunately, however, reality is different. Resignation and mourning for good friends, killed when their Ju 87 was shot down.

The German Messer-schmitt Bf 109 E, F, and G fighter aircraft, as well as the Italian Macchi 200 and 202 fighters bore the brunt of the air battles over North Africa.

Generalmajor Fröhlich, from 20 February 1941 "Fliegerführer Afrika" (lit. "leader of pilots in Africa") seen at the Tmimi airfield in conversation with *Oblt.* Jacob of 4/StG 2, who was later awarded the Knight's Cross. In the center is *Major* Enneccerus, commander of II/StG 2, whose Gruppe enjoyed outstanding success against the British naval and merchant fleets in the Mediterranean.

Ofw. Heller of III/ZG 26 poses in front of the rudder of his Bf 110, which already carries markings of five air victories. He scored three of these kills during a single mission on 15 July 1941. On this mission, he was acting as a pathfinder for II/StG 2 attacking ships on the North African coast. During the flight, the Gruppe was jumped by 14 British fighters with only Heller opposing them. In the ensuing dogfight he shot down three of the Curtiss fighters, broke up the enemy formation, and brought the Stukas safely home without suffering a single loss. For this action he was awarded the Knight's Cross on 21 August 1941, after his total had risen to eight kills.

Tmimi, summer 1941: The "Cäsar" (a Ju 87R) of *Lt.* Pölz from 6/StG 2 with an eye-catching paint job. The snake stretched across the entire length of the fuselage.

"Achtung - Stuka!"

Whenever the alarm "Stuka!" was sounded during the Second World War, it meant fear and terror for the enemy. But friendly ground forces found this to be an expression of relief, welcome help in a tricky situation or much-needed support during an attack. This cry was heard throughout the African theater, in all hotspots and on many Allied military and merchant ships in the Mediterranean area. The legendary Junkers Ju 87 "Sturzkampfflugzeug" (dive bomber), known during the War and today simply as the "Stuka", made headlines in this theater as well.

Following the heavy losses suffered during the Battle of Britain and the subsequent replenishment, the Stuka units were transferred to Sicily at the beginning of 1941. From here they first flew missions against sea targets in the Med and against Malta — with notable success. On 10 January 1941, II/StG 2 "Immelmann" under *Major* Enneccerus and I/StG 1 under *Hptm.* Hozzell flew a well-executed attack against the British aircraft carrier "Illustrious", which was so severely damaged by six direct hits that it was only able to reach the docks in Malta with the greatest of difficulties. In Malta's harbor of La Valetta it was hit again, but the British were nevertheless able to get the "Illustrious" to Alexandria. However, the carrier had suffered so much damage that it was out of commission for a year and had to be repaired in America. One day later II/StG 2, under the leadership of *Major* Enneccerus, succeeded in sinking the 10000 ton British cruiser "Southampton" and in doing so, once again demonstrated the effectiveness of Stuka operations against even the most modern of warships.

In continued operations in the Mediterranean, the Stuka enjoyed considerable success in attacks on Malta as well as during operations against Allied convoys and warship fleets. The Italians, too, distinguished themselves in these operations. Not only were their torpedo bomber units effective, but also their dive bomber units (mostly ranging from squadron to group strength), which were equipped with the German-supplied Ju 87 (known by the Italians as the "Pichiatello").

Beginning in February of 1941 II/StG 2 and I/StG 1 were also used in North Africa, providing valuable support to Rommel's DAK. Aside from these two Gruppen, the following Stuka units also flew in Africa: Stab, I, II, and III Gruppe of StG 3, and III/StG 1. II/StG 2 "Immelmann" flew here from February 1941 to December 1942, making it the longest-operating Stuka unit in the theater. Individual Staffeln from various Gruppen also participated in Tunisia (e.g. 6/StG 3 under *Lt.* Pölz).

All the Stuka units proved themselves in an outstanding manner during the ever-changing conflict in Africa. Stuka Geschwader 3, under *Oberstlt.* Sigel, was simply called the Africa Geschwader, since it had been in that theater with its Stab and all three Gruppen for such a long time. Among other things, the Stukas struck at fortified positions and operated on the tank battlefield with repeated success. The fall of Tobruk in June of 1942 is a prime example of the cooperation achieved between tanks and Stukas. In order for the operation to succeed, Fort Bir Hacheim would have to first be rendered ineffective. On 9 June 1942, more than a hundred Ju 87 Stukas under the command of *Oberstlt.* Sigel attacked this key position in two waves, thereby paving the way for the successful capture of the fort two days later. This was, however, the largest number of Stukas employed during any single operation in the North African campaign. Usually the Stuka units only had 40-70 aircraft at their disposal; very often the number was much less. This was due to the heavy losses suffered at the hands of the successful British fighter and anti-aircraft defenses, as well as the constant shortage of pilots, aircraft, fuel and other material. For example, at the end of 1942 there were only 60 Stukas which were fit for combat in the entire Mediterranean region (10 in Sicily, 20 in Tunisia, and 30 in North Africa during Rommel's retreat)!

In spite of the oppressive Allied air superiority, the Stuka units were still able to inflict damage on the enemy. Flying 360 sorties in close cooperation with fighters and the outstanding attack pilots of the newly-formed I/SchG 2 (equipped with the Hs 129 and Bf 109 fighter-bomber), Stukas caused considerable losses among the Allies during the offensive at Feriana and Sbeitla on 14 February 1943. In spite of the success, however, these local victories had little influence on the outcome of the campaign.

At the end of April 1943 the few remaining Ju 87 Stukas were transferred back to Sicily.

Right page:
Engulfed in a thick cloud of dust, the Stukas take off and join up in a picturesque formation. These planes are bound for a strike against the harbor of Tobruk.

Right page:
Their success is reflected in these excellent photos taken by the reconnaissance aircraft after the mission; the German term "versenkt" indicates those ships which were sunk.

Shortly before the target the formation loosens up somewhat in preparation for their dive on the ships in the harbor.

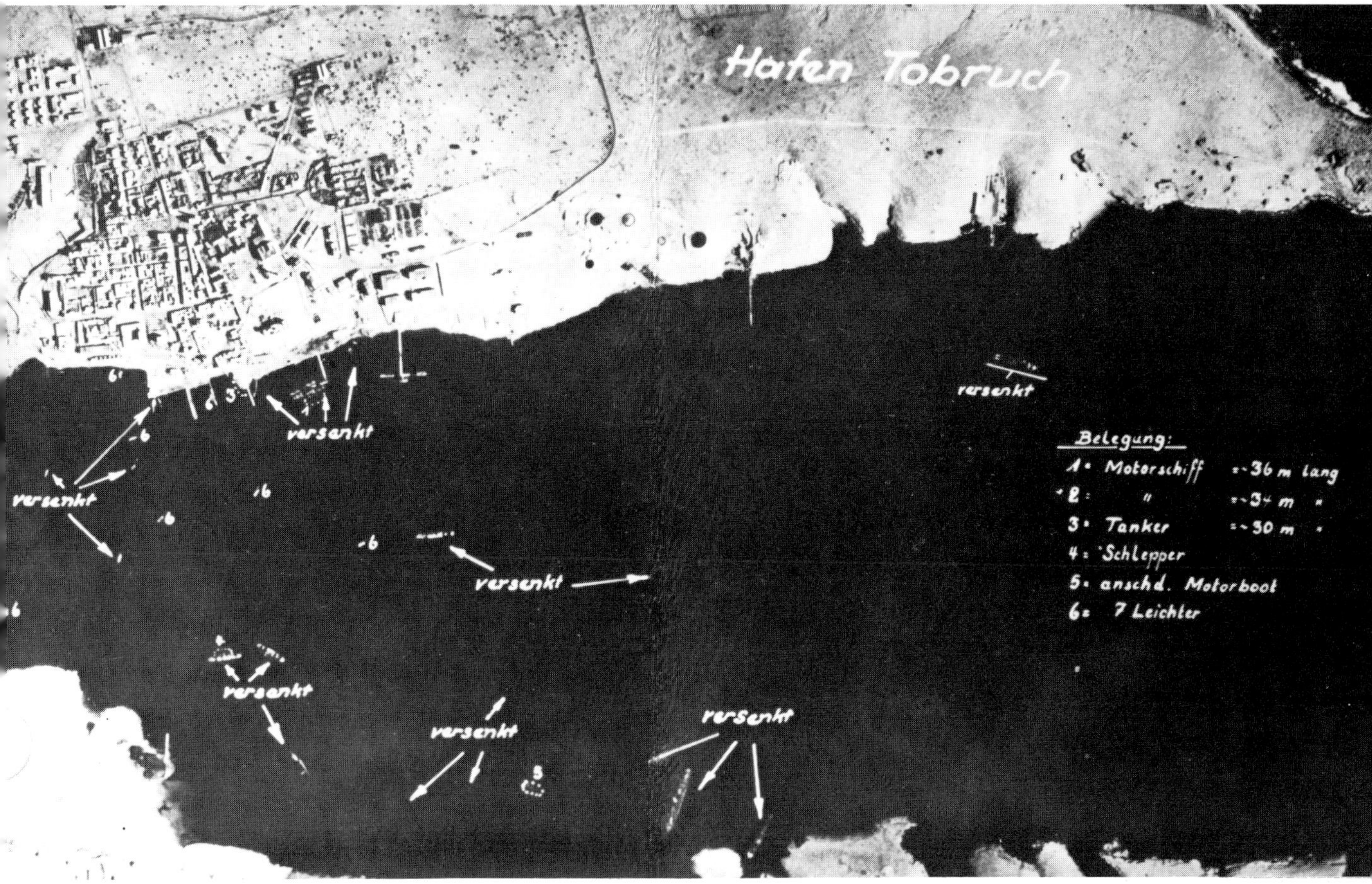
Hafen Tobruch
versenkt
versenkt
versenkt
versenkt
versenkt
versenkt
versenkt
Belegung:
1 = Motorschiff =~36 m lang
2 = " =~34 m "
3 = Tanker =~30 m "
4 = Schlepper
5 = anschd. Motorboot
6 = 7 Leichter

Hptm. "Edu" Neumann, commander of the I/JG 27 and later commander of the Geschwader, accompanies *GeneralMajor* Fröhlich to his automobile following a situational briefing.

The Gruppe standard posted in front of the command post.

Nearby are the aircraft, parked in the sweltering heat of Africa. In the center is "White 1", the aircraft of *Oblt.* Redlich (1 Staffel's commander), whose rudder already displays the markings of 20 kills.

The bomber units are also operating around the clock, and are primarily used against shipping targets. These pictures, taken at the Heraklion airfield on Crete, show the Ju 88's heavy bombs and the special anti-shipping PC-RS 1400kg bomb.

Hptm. Helbig, the Staffelkapitan of 4/(Kampf-)LG 1, seen taking off in Eleusis for an anti-shipping strike with the special bomb mounted externally.

Ju 88 A-5, LG+GM of the 4/(Kampf-)LG 1 seen here approaching a British convoy. Two 500kg bombs and a single 1000kg bomb are mounted externally on hardpoints.

The ships are caught in a hail of bombs, which this time have missed their target.

A crew of the I Gruppe of LG 1 in Eleusis standing in front of the rudder of their Ju 88, which carries a notable victory balance. The painted-on bomb explosions indicate hits, while the ships with a "V" and the tonnage indicate sinkings.

Lt. Gerhard Stamp of the 2/(Kampf-)LG 1 checks out a "sunk ship emblem" with a ground crewman. The marking represents a large British destroyer, which Stamp caught between Malta and Crete and sent to the bottom on 11 July 1941.

Another of the famous "ship killers" of LG 1 was *Oblt.* Iro Ilk (second from right, wearing the Knight's Cross). In 1943 he transferred to fighters and rose to *Major* and commander of III/JG 300 "Wilde Sau" before losing his life in a dogfight with Spitfires during the defense of the Reich on 25 August 1944.

Much ado in Eleusis for a Ju 88 crew of the III/KG 30 just returning from their 100th combat mission.

Hptm. Helbig, commander of the 4th Staffel of LG 1, returns from a maintenance flight with his crew chief Behm. The aircraft is seen taxiing in Eleusis following an engine change.

Ofw. Richard Heller was one of the great aces among the German Zerstörer pilots. He remained with his Staffel (8/ZG 26) even after being awarded the Knight's Cross and continued to serve with his companions, relentlessly flying bombing missions, escort, reconnaissance, and fighter sweeps.

Impressive photographs showing a Stuka attack on a British freighter, which was sunk off the North African coast.

Ju 87 B-2, TG+FN of the II/StG 2 on operational sortie, bound for Tobruk (left). The Stuka formation begins its dive on British anti-aircraft positions surrounding the fortress of Tobruk. As the aircraft egress from the target, the clouds from the explosions testify to the effectiveness of their strike.

During the summer of 1941 7/JG 26 also participated briefly in the conflict in Africa.

Scramble! Leaving a gigantic trail of dust, a Bf 109 takes off from the airfield to intercept the enemy.

Still burning, the remains of a British fighter lie at the edge of the airfield following a vicious dogfight.

On 8 September 1941, *Oblt.* Hogeback, Staffelkapitän of 9/(Kampf-)LG 1, was awarded the Knight's Cross in Derna by *Generalmajor* Fröhlich. After 163 combat missions over Poland, on the Western Front, over England and the Channel, in the Balkans, in the Mediterranean, and in North Africa, this was truly a well-deserved decoration.

A Ju 88 of 2/(Kampf-)LG 1 photographed shortly after takeoff from Crete, setting off on an armed reconnaissance mission. The aircraft is camouflaged in "Mediterranean flora (machia)."

Gefreiter Arnold Huebner, a gunner from 3/FlaRgt 33 (mot.), was awarded the Knight's Cross for destroying no less than 24 enemy tanks. 16 of these, as well as the annihilation of an artillery battery, occurred during the Battle of Sollum in June 1941.

Above right: These 88mm anti-aircraft guns were not only used for engaging ground targets but were also used to provide protection against aircraft. They've taken up position at the edge of an important supply harbor.

Command position and equipment of a heavy 88mm anti-aircraft battery.

Again and again, the Stukas fall upon the enemy's bunkers, anti-aircraft positions, troop concentrations, docks, and ships in the city and harbor of Tobruk and its surroundings.

During these missions, the Stuka units continued to suffer losses at the hands of heavy anti-aircraft and fighter defenses. This crew of 3/StG 3 was fortunate. Wounded and forced to land in the desert, they were able to make their way back to their own lines after a period of several days. Even after being medically treated, the men still bear the scars of their ordeal as they pose for the camera following the presentation of the Iron Cross II by the commander of StG 3, *Oberstlt.* Sigel (left). To the right is their Staffelkapitän, Wearer of the Knight's Cross *Oblt.* Naumann.

A proud day for the (Kampf-) Lehrgeschwader 1. The beginning of September 1941 saw *Ofw.* Schlund receive the Knight's Cross from his commander, *Major* Knust, at the airfield in Eleusis. When he was officially awarded the Cross on 30 August 1941, he became the first radioman in the Luftwaffe to wear this high honor. He had flown over 200 missions, had three aerial victories to his credit, and played a major role in the successes of *Hptm.* Helbig (seen on the right in the upper picture).

Right page:
Just one day after the big celebration it was back to flying combat missions. Seen here shortly before takeoff (from left to right) is *Lt.* Sauer, Staffel officer and successful pilot of 4/(Kampf-)LG 1 — missing in action since 21 October 1941 — *Hptm.* Helbig and *Ofw.* Schlund, the new Wearer of the Knight's Cross. In the lower picture (to the right next to Schlund) is the rear gunner of Helbig's crew, *Feldwebel* Cirpka.

While the bomber and dive bomber pilots continued to fulfill their missions, the Messerschmitt fighters of JG 27 were constantly in the air, trying to wrest the air superiority over the desert from the powerful and numerically superior enemy.

Homeward bound. Ju 87 B-2s of II/StG 2 are seen returning to their home airfield from a mission.

A Stuka attack on a British fleet in the Mediterranean, as portrayed by a propaganda artist.

Beginning in the summer of 1941 German bombers, primarily from LG 1, flew from Crete to conduct evening and night attacks on the harbor city of Alexandria. The brunt of these attacks on the single most important supply point for the British fleet was borne by the harbor itself, the railyards and oil storage areas. The oil facilities, so vital to the fleet as a fuel source, were seriously damaged by bomb hits. This aerial photo from a German reconnaissance plane provides a good view of Alexandria's West Harbor, the British fleet's base.

Right page:
Hptm. Helbig also flew missions against Alexandria with his Staffel (4/LG 1). The photo shows him during a mission briefing with his men. From right to left *Major* Stephan, radioman *Ofw.* Schlund, *Lt.* Sauer and his radioman, *Hptm.* Helbig and *Feldwebel* Cirpka. The lower photograph also shows *Feldwebel* Behm (in black overalls), Helbig's crew chief. Particularly noteworthy in this photo is the fact that the Ju 88's underside has been smeared with soot (!) to mask against searchlights and moonlight.

3U
R

Left page:
Above: Bf 110s of III/ZG 26 on a mission to conduct low-level strikes against British troop and vehicle concentrations.

Below: This aircraft took several hits during the attack. With difficulty, the crew managed to reach German lines. Italian Askaris are seen here guarding the wreck.

Reconnaissance crews had it rough on both sides. Due to the nature of their missions, fighter defenses concentrated particularly on them. The above picture shows a Maryland I of 60 (South African) Squadron prior to a recon mission. Below is the Ju 88 of *Hptm.* Muggenthaler of 1(F)/121, Wearer of the Knight's Cross. Following a mission over Africa, Muggenthaler barely managed to reach the coast of Crete, where he made an emergency landing.

The transport units and their Ju 52s (seen here are Ju 52/3m aircraft of III/KGzbV 1) unceasingly brought in troop supplies, weapons and other goods across the Med to Africa. Their exemplary performance deserves the highest praise.

Camouflage and cover are necessary in Africa, too. This Bf 109 of I/JG 27 is seen parked in one of the revetments typical for this theater.

Leaving the typical trail of billowing dust, this Messerschmitt fighter taxis out for takeoff.

Two particularly impressive photos showing a desert scramble by a Staffel of I/JG 27.

Along the African coast — and against the enemy! The bombs can be clearly seen under the wings of these Ju 87s. (left) *Right:* Marmarika, November 1941: Using their guns and bombs, Stuka bombers of the Headquarters (Stab) Staffel of II/StG 2 peel off to begin their attack on the British Army's supply depot at Tajab el Esem (right). *Below:* 26 November 1941 at the Tmimi airfield: a high-level dignitary pays a visit to the successful Stuka pilots of II/StG 2. From left to right: Nachrichtenoffizier (intelligence officer) *Lt.* Behnke, *Lt.* Pölz, *Oblt.* Hamester, *Generalfeldmarschall* Kesselring and *General der Flieger* Geisler.

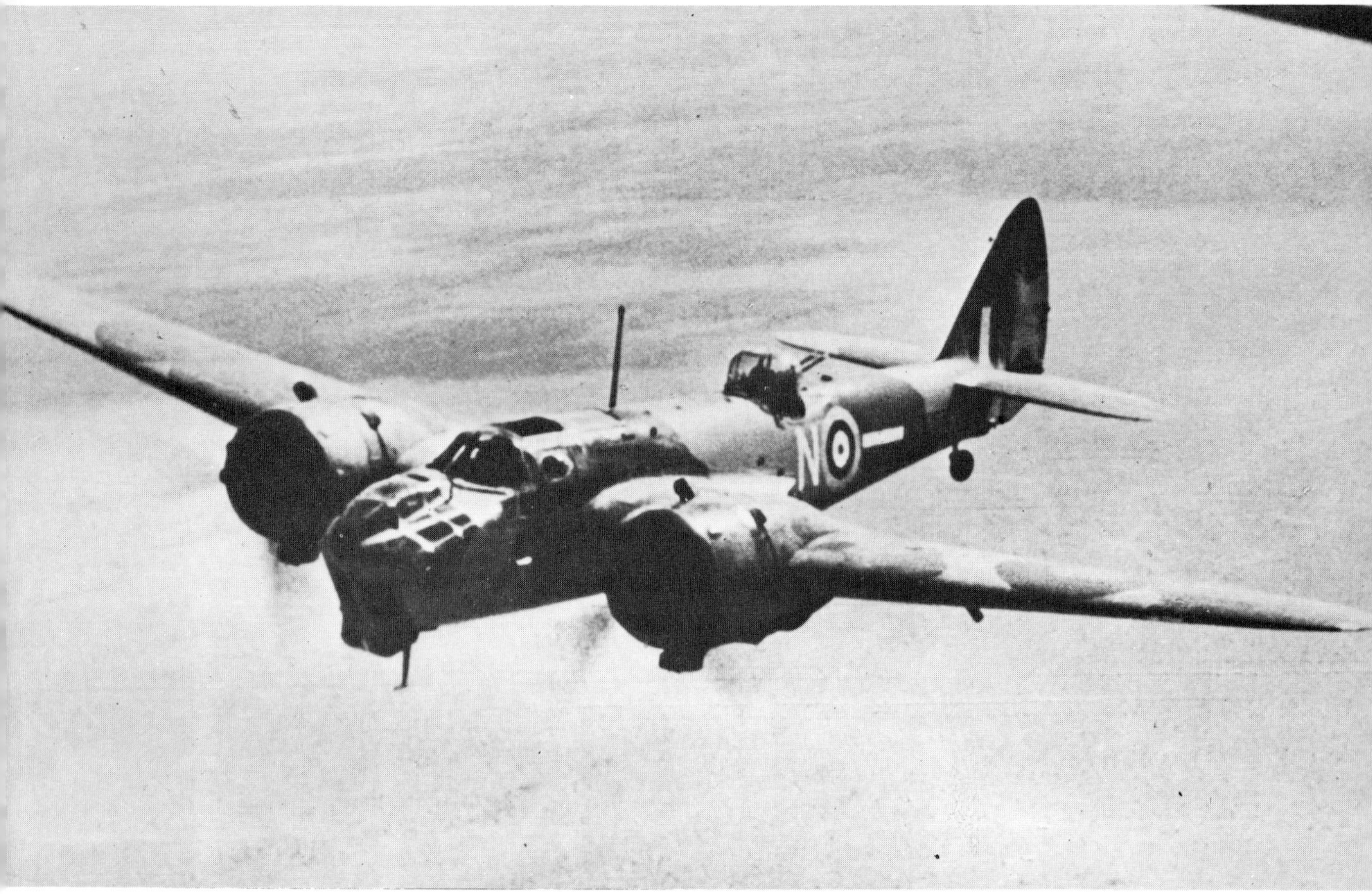
N

Left page:
A Bristol Blenheim IV of 14 Squadron on an operational sortie over the Libyan Desert — and below, after being shot down by German fighters.

Again and again, the Stukas brought aid and relief to their comrades on the ground, who by now were having to fight on the defensive. These are seen preparing to attack British tanks near Ghobi. The relative number of Stukas deployed was quite high, given the type of theater Africa was considered to be.

Now it was the turn of British tanks and trucks in the area of Sollum. After pulling up from the strike, the aircraft crews could see bomb explosions for kilometers.

On 13 December 1941 JG 27 suffered a major loss. *Ofw.* Albert Espenlaub, one of the most popular and successful (with 14 kills) members of 1 Staffel, was hit in his aircraft's radiator and forced to land near El Adem. He was captured alive by the British, but on the same day he attempted to escape and was shot to death.

A Rotte of Bf 109s confidently overflies their own airfield. In the foreground on the right is a familiar sight, a now legendary VW Kübelwagen Type 82 and a captured British tent.

An officer's conference at II/StG 2 in Tmimi in December 1941. From left to right: *Lt.* Heim, *Lt.* Pölz, *Oblt.* Jacob, *General der Flieger* Geisler and *Hptm.* Busselt.

An engine change and repair on a Ju 87 B-2. The "blackmen" in this theater performed their job under the most difficult conditions and often only had the most primitive tools at their disposal.

Left: **Rommel with a concerned look on his face. The British winter offensive (18 November 1941 - 5 January 1942) has not yet been fully repelled. On the left is the Chief of Staff of Panzer Gruppe Afrika, *Generalmajor* Gause.**

Right: **The first Christmas holiday for the German soldiers on the African continent is rapidly approaching. This Luftwaffe soldier has spent his free time tenderly working on his gift from Africa for those loved ones back home.**

Christmas Eve in the desert. Wherever possible, members of the Luftwaffe celebrate the holiday with a few meaningful hours — in spite of the retreat and the critical situation.

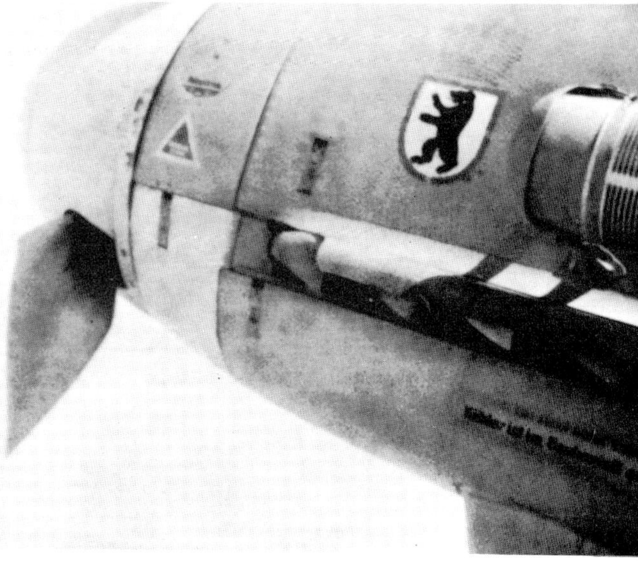

In 1942 JG 27 also bore the brunt of the air campaign over the desert. Since December of the previous year all three Gruppen and the Geschwader headquarters unit had been in Africa. The Geschwader rapidly became known as the Afrika Geschwader and remained for almost two years on the Dark Continent. During this time it racked up impressive victories — and paid a heavy price for them.

From November of 1941 until August 1942 I/NJG 2 was also used in Africa. They flew effective day and night missions from both airfields in Sicily and Crete as well as from various fields in North Africa. The photo above shows a Ju 88 C-2 of the Gruppe parked at an African forward airfield. In the picture below note that the Ju 88s also carried the white recognition bands on the wings.

Oblt. Heinz-Horst Hissbach of I/NJG 2 seen here with his crew following his 100th operational mission. He was killed by anti-aircraft fire after 34 night victories on 14 April 1945 during a night low level attack on an American supply column.

Ju 87 R-2 aircraft fly in a loose formation along the North African coast. The Gruppe's emblem can clearly be discerned on the engine cowling; it is a drawing of Wilhelm Busch's raven "Hans Huckebein."

Stukas attack! This is how a Luftwaffe war artist envisions a Stuka attack during the tank battles in Africa.

The British have captured this damaged Ju 87 B-2 of 3/StG 1. Notice the yellow-brown camouflage, liberally spattered with green.

The He 111s of II/KG 26 "Löwengeschwader" also became a more frequent participant in the war in Africa. Here are two impressive photos, one showing the takeoff of an He 111 and the other a combat mission with heavy bombs.

The courageous crewmen of the He 111s enjoyed considerable success in operations against Malta and shipping targets, as well as on strikes carried out against shipping in the Suez Canal and the Red Sea.

In spite of taking an anti-aircraft hit in the right wing, this Bf 110 of III/ZG 26 managed to make it back from a mission to Malta and land at its home airfield of Catania on Sicily. The pilot, wearing a life preserver, can be seen on the left.

Bf 110s of 8/ZG 26 provide air cover for a convoy; they are seen here overflying one of the Italian escort ships.

The Ju 52s of the transport units fly tirelessly over the Mediterranean, bringing Rommel and his soldiers urgently needed supplies.

On 21 January 1942 *Hptm.* Theo Blaich — seen here as an *Oberleutnant* at the rudder of his famous Bf 108 "Taifun" (notice the patched anti-aircraft holes, reminders of a flight over Tobruk) flew one of the most daring missions of the Luftwaffe in Africa. Together with *Lt.* Bohnsack, *Fw.* Geissler, *Uffz.* Wichmann, war reporter *Lt.* Dettmann and the Italian Major Conte Vimercat-Sanverino, he attacked Fort Lamy on Lake Chad — a one-way distance of some 2500 kilometers. 400,000 liters of aviation fuel and the entire supply of oil went up in smoke, and ten aircraft were destroyed. The fort was put out of commission for weeks. On the return flight the fuel ran out and Blaich had to make an emergency landing in the desert. On 27 January an Italian Ghibli S 1 reconnaissance aircraft spotted the crew and brought them water. The next day all were rescued by *Oblt.* Becker flying a Ju 52 of the Wüstennotstaffel. Eight days after setting out on their adventure the men and their He 111 finally returned to their starting point, the tiny Italian forward airfield on Campo Uno.

View of central Africa's Lake Chad from the He 111 as it approaches Fort Lamy. In the southeastern and eastern parts, the lake is characterized primarily by huge groups of islands. The Sahara had long ago begun to eat its way into this area.

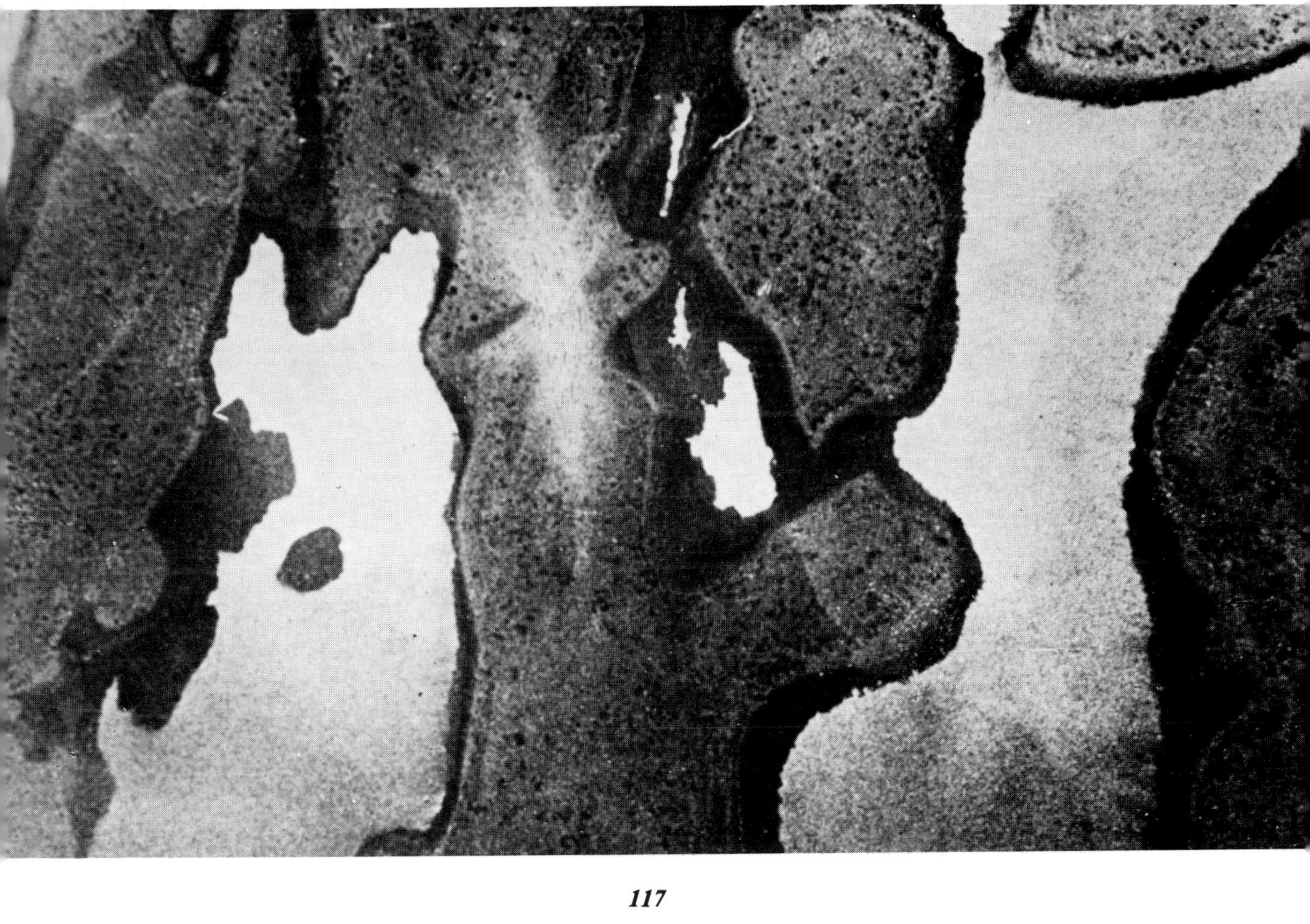

Daily operations at a supply airfield in Sicily.

A Curtiss P-40 Kittyhawk of 112 Squadron, with its shark mouth and 250 pound bomb with an impact fuse. Aircraft of this type were effectively used by the Allies in Africa as fighter-bombers and low-level attack aircraft.

British aircraft have set this Ju 52 on fire during a strafing attack. Once again, the troops lose valuable supplies and a transport plane.

WATCHERS OVER SAND AND SEA

The flying reconnaissance units of the German Luftwaffe (strategic and tactical reconnaissance, weather and courier services) had an extremely difficult time in the North African campaign and during operations in the Mediterranean region. Their numbers were few, yet the demands that were placed upon them in this theater were particularly high. Nearly always operating alone, the crews were subject to extreme physical and psychological stress, especially over the battlefield and as they ranged behind enemy lines or over the sea. In addition, they had to deal with weather conditions with which they were not familiar, conditions which played a major role in reconnoitering the vast expanse of North Africa and the Mediterranean. Sand and heat — two concepts which form an integral part of the word "desert" — made life particularly difficult for the strategic reconnaissance pilots in North Africa. During the summer months, the pilots had to deal with temperatures which fluctuated as much as 80 degrees Celsius between takeoff and landing. The heat not only tested the mettle of every man, but also thinned the air so much that the normal operating altitudes for reconnaissance simply could not be reached. In order to fulfill their missions, the crews were therefore forced to fly at altitudes which put them within range of the medium-size anti-aircraft guns — especially during the African summer.

Navigation also presented a severe problem, since there are few marked orientation points in the desert; on the sea there are none whatsoever. The few oases, settlements and forts scattered across the desert were much easier to find on the map than in reality, where one looked pretty much the same as another and offered little opportunity for orientation.

However, all this and the constant threat posed by the massive enemy fighter and anti-aircraft defenses did not prevent the reconnaissance pilots from successfully carrying out their many responsibilities. They continued to fly their missions over the Med, often for several hours at a time, reconnoitered over Malta, Alexandria as well as the Suez Canal. Primarily using aerial photography, they flew day and night, providing operational reconnaissance for the upper echelons of command, tactical reconnaissance for the mid-level commanders, and target reconnaissance for the attacking units on the ground and in the air.

Tactical reconnaissance units — primarily equipped with single-seaters — had to monitor the rapid movements of the ground forces, the speed of which was enhanced by the common use of tank as well as other motorized units. If the reconnaissance data was to be of any value at all, the pilots needed to report the results to headquarters immediately.

The pilots flew their missions and provided effective aerial reconnaissance of the preparations, conduct and breakoff of combat, of the terrain, approach and strength distribution of the enemy. Without them, the many successful defensive and offensive operations conducted by Rommel and his men would not have been possible.

At various times from 1941 to 1943, the following aerial reconnaissance units operated in the North African campaign, Tunisia, and the Mediterranean region:

2(H)/14

4(H)/12

1(F)/121
Stab, 1st and 2nd Staffel of Aufkl.Gr. (F)/122
2(F)/123
Luftbild-Staffel 1
Wettererkundungs-Staffel 26
1/KüFl.Gr.406
3/KüFl.Gr.506
2/Kü.Fl.Gr.906
2/Seeaufkl.Gr.125
3/Seeaufkl.Gr.125
Stab, 1-3/Seeaufkl.Gr.126
Lufttransportstaffel See 222
Wettererkundungs-Staffel 27

The following order of the day (tagesbefehl) from the commanding general of X Fliegerkorps, *General der Flieger* Geisler, represents the performance and sacrifice of all members of the aerial reconnaissance units who served in Africa.

From the commanding general of X Fliegerkorps
Headquarters, 29 June 1941

KORPSTAGESBEFEHL:
To the crew
Oberleutnant Felgenhauer, pilot
Feldwebel Zieslak, radioman
Gefreiter Groeschel, gunner

of 2(F)/123, who for the fourth time now have succeeded in carrying out their mission and delivering the results in a timely manner, in spite of a seriously damaged aircraft. On two of these missions they were forced to fly for several hours on a single engine. The performance is due to the bravery, the excellent flying ability and the exemplary cooperation of the crew.

On two flights each, the crew was also accompanied by the commander of the Gruppe, Major von Obernitz, and Oberleutnant Augustin as observers.

I would like to offer my highest regards to the crew, especially the pilot for his skillful and brave conduct, and to Major von Obernitz for the successful completion of the missions.

Geisler

Lt. Paul Felder, pilot from the 1(F)/AufklGr 121, sits in his cockpit shortly before taking off on an operational sortie. The nose of his Ju 88 carries the Staffel insignia, a symbol familiar to all fliers in Africa.

A particularly impressive photo of the island of Malta, taken from an altitude of approximately 7500 meters.

One of the best crews of 1(F)/AufklGr 121 poses here after their 100th operational mission. The commander and observer *Oblt.* Muggenthaler stands second from left, while third from left is *Lt.* Felder, the pilot. Both were awarded the Knight's Cross for providing exceptional photographic data, which they took while flying under the most difficult operational and weather conditions in Africa and over the Med.

The boss — Staffelkapitän *Oblt.* Erwin Fischer (on the far right) — has just landed, and relates to his comrades his latest air combat where a Spitfire pursued him for 25 minutes and unsuccessfully tried to shoot his plane down.

The board of honor of 1(F)/AufklärungsGruppe 121, showing its members who have been awarded the Knight's Cross.

A rare photograph showing a German strategic reconnaissance aircraft under attack at high altitudes by an enemy fighter.

Ju 88s of (Kampf-) Lehrgeschwader 1 attack a British truck convoy.

A Schwarm of Messerschmitt fighters take off on a combat mission.

Right: After 50 kills (7 over the Channel, the remainder in Africa), *Lt.* Marseille of 3/JG 27 was awarded the Knight's Cross on 22 February 1942. His outstanding vision and unique shooting ability made him a truly exceptional pilot, even among the many excellent pilots in the German Luftwaffe.

"Jochen" Marseille's famous "Yellow 14", here Bf 109F W.Nr. 8693, being refueled. His victory tally at that time can be seen on the aircraft's rudder.

"Freie Jagd", or a fighter sweep over the field of combat. Shown here on the prowl is the 1st Staffel of JG 27 flying in loose formation.

After a mission it's back to the tents and bunkers at the airfield. From left to right in this picture: von Lieres und Wilkau, Körner, unknown and Franzisket, all from I/JG 27.

A great snapshot showing a Bf 109 of I/JG 27 taxiing out for takeoff.

The men of I Gruppe of JG 27 were known for their humor. The entire Gruppe was sometimes jokingly referred to as "Neumann's Variety Show." Aside from the commander's circus trailer, this ancient vehicle also belonged to the Gruppe's motor pool. The sign reads "Not For Sale." In the picture from left to right: *Oblt.* Keller, *Hptm.* Homuth and *Lt.* Remmer.

Here's another section of the interior of "Edu" Neumann's trailer, showing the famous 1000 African natives. Already 35 palm fronds cover *Oblt.* Redlich's "native", while that of *Oblt.* Framm wears eight (a frond is added for every kill).

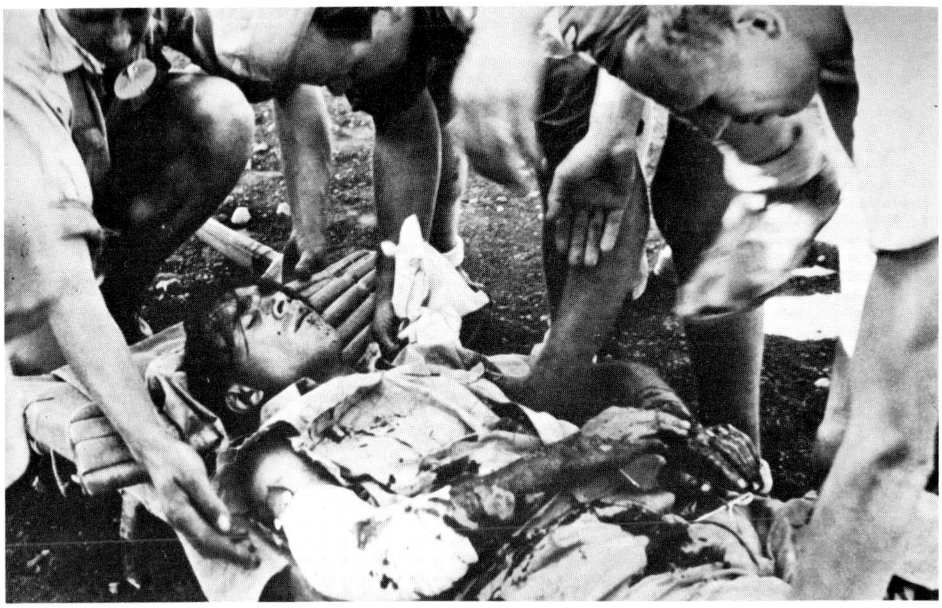

Two dramatic photos which weren't carried by the media during the Second World War. Comrades pull a critically wounded gunner from a Bf 110. In this case the man is a war reporter for the Luftwaffe who suffered his injuries fending off a British fighter attack. Evidence which shows how even the reporters and photojournalists placed their lives in jeopardy on the front lines, often for a single report or a few meters of film.

Constant danger existed not only in the air, but also on the ground. *Ofw.* Jaculli, *Hptm.* Christl's trusty radioman (on the right, next to Christl), lost his life in such a manner when the airfield was strafed and bombed by the British.

Yet another photograph which portrays the horrors of war in all its grisly truth: A German rescue detail removes the charred remains of a British tanker from the wreckage of his vehicle, destroyed by an 88mm anti-aircraft gun.

The Bf 110's drop tanks permitted the aircraft to fly deep into the enemy's rear areas. Aircraft of III/ZG 26 make a diving attack on British supply facilities.

Oblt. Schulze-Dickow, Staffelkapitän of 8/ZG 26 and from 12 July 1943 *Hptm.* Christl's successor as commander of the famous III/ZG 26. He, too, was considered one of the great aces among the Zerstörer pilots.

Hptm. Christl (left), commander of III/ZG 26 seen here during a mission briefing on Sicily shortly before another flight to Africa. In the first row (third from left) stands *Ofw.* Heller, who was awarded the Knight's Cross to the Iron Cross on 21 August 1941.

Hptm. Christl (right), seen conversing with *Generalleutnant* Hoffmann von Waldau. As "Fliegerführer Afrika", von Waldau succeeded *Generalleutnant* Stefan Fröhlich as commander of Luftwaffe operations in the North African theater.

High-level visitor at III/ZG 26 in the desert. *Generalfeldmarschall* Kesselring often paid visits to his Luftwaffe units on the front lines. He not only ensured that the units were kept in the best possible state of operational readiness, but also looked after the personal welfare of the men — as far as this was possible.

Following a low-level attack on his own airfield by 20 British fighters, *Ofw.* Otto Schulz of 4/JG 27 managed to scramble his plane in less than 30 seconds. Within ten minutes he shot down five of the attacking aircraft (all Kittyhawks of 94 and 112 Squadron). The photo shows two of his kills, the columns of smoke from their explosions marking the edge of the airfield.

Ofw. Otto Schulz stands in front of his Bf 109 F. After 332 combat missions during which he shot down 44 aircraft, he was awarded the Knight's Cross on 22 February 1942. But the desert also claimed him, one of the most skilled fighter pilots in Africa. Following his 51st victory (45th in Africa alone), he fell to his death after a dogfight with Kittyhawks on 17 June 1942 near Sidi Rezegh.

The armorers and mechanics did their job in the baking sun, often working in temperatures over 50 degrees Celsius. Their efforts were never mentioned in any OKW report, yet they remain forever in the hearts of the pilots and crew; thanks to them the aircrews were able to achieve their successes, and many owed their lives to the ground crewmen.

Martuba, 30 March 1942. *Oblt.* Rudi Sinner of II/JG 27 sits on the wing of his Bf 109 F, flanked by his two ground crewmen.

General der Jagdflieger Adolf Galland, pays a visit to his fighters in North Africa. Galland (on the left) is seen here conversing with *Hptm.* Neumann.

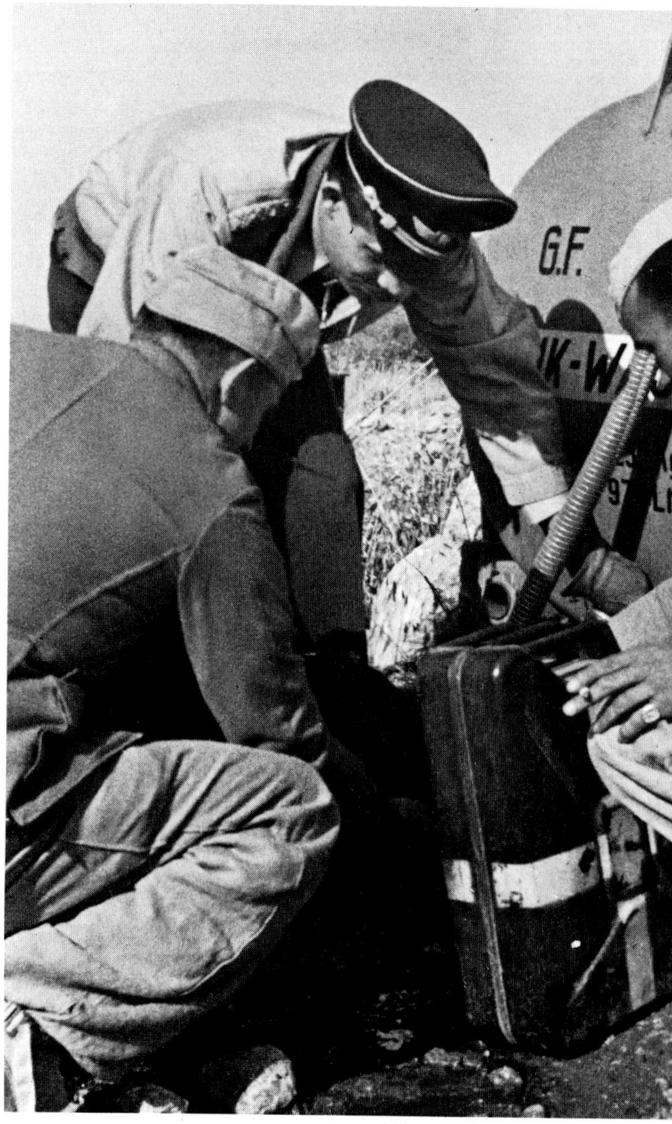

Galland checks a tank truck and water canister, both common items in the African theater.

Bomber Pilots in North Africa

In December 1940, *General der Flieger* Geisler's X Fliegerkorps was transferred from Norway to Sicily. The corps was tasked to "strike against escorted British convoys in the Mediterranean, the British access through the Suez Canal, and to prevent the advance of the British army in Libya." After the Deutsches Afrikakorps landed, it was also given the responsibility of protecting the DAK's sea transport routes from Italy to Tripoli, as well as to carry out attacks against the island fortress of Malta. The X Fliegerkorps had approximately 330 aircraft available at that time, of which roughly 120 were bombers of various types (none were Ju 87 "Stukas", however).

On the recommendation of *Major* i.G. (im Generalstab, or of the General Staff) Harlinghausen, the Chief of Staff for X Fliegerkorps, II/KG 26 ("Löwengeschwader") under *Major* Bertram flew from Comiso in Sicily to Benghazi, and from there took off on 17 January 1941 to strike a convoy in the Suez Canal that had been sighted by reconnaissance aircraft. In flying this strike, II/KG 26 became the first bomber unit to fly a mission in North Africa.

During the more than two year struggle for North Africa, Malta and Tunisia, several different bomber units were involved in attaining the goals named above, as well as many other objectives which appeared as the campaign progressed. While the duration of operations varied from one bomber unit to the next, all those listed below participated in the theater at one time or another:

- Kampf-Lehrgeschwader 1 with Stab, I, II, and III Gruppe
- KG 1 "Hindenburg" with Stab, I, and II Gruppe
- 2/KG 4 "General Wever" as a Minenstaffel, as well as I and II Gruppe
- KG 6 with parts of Stab, I and II Gruppe
- KG 26 "Löwengeschwader" with Stab, I, II and III Gruppe
- KG 30 "Adler-Geschwader" with Stab, I, II and III Gruppe
- 9/KG 40 (operating Fw 200 "Condor" aircraft)
- KG 54 with Stab, I, III (formerly K.Gr. 806) and IV Gruppe
- KG 76 with Stab, I and II Gruppe, as well as parts of III Gruppe
- KG 77 with Stab, II and III Gruppe
- II/KG 100 (formerly III/KG 26) and 7/KG 100
- Kü.Fl.Gr. 606 (from 10 Sept. 1942 renamed I/KG 77 and continuing to operate in the Mediterranean region)
- Korpskette X Flieger-Korps (Harlinghausen)

As mentioned previously, the duration of operations in the African theater fluctuated considerably from unit to unit, ranging from one month to over two years. During the course of the campaign, one of the oldest and best Kampfgeschwader in the Luftwaffe, Kampf-Lehrgeschwader 1, came to be considered *the* Mediterranean Geschwader as well as the Afrika Geschwader. This unit, equipped with the Ju 88, was labeled "the fire department" of the Mediterranean, a title which was justly deserved. The following brief synopsis of KLG 1's 1941-1943 operations in the Mediterranean are representative of all bomber units operating in this area: Malta, Rommel's offensives and retreats in Africa/Egypt, Balkans campaign, Crete, Mediterranean convoys, mining of the Suez Canal, Tobruk, El Alamein, Suez/Haifa, Port Said, Alexandria, the invasion of Algeria, Sicily, Salerno/Naples, Leros and Nettuno-Anzio.

The most famous unit of KLG 1 was I Gruppe, led by *Major* Joachim Helbig, who later became the Geschwaderkommodore. They were called the "Helbig Flyers", and were well-known and feared by the enemy. Helbig, who was awarded the Knight's Cross with Oak Leaves and Swords on 28 Sept. 1942, flew Ju 88 "L1+AM (later AMB)" for over three years. With approximately 1100 flight hours on the airframe, of which over 750 were combat hours, this was the most famous Ju 88 in the German Luftwaffe. It was only flown by Helbig and his personal crew, and no other Ju 88 ever reached this number of flight hours. Unfortunately, this nearly legendary aircraft was destroyed by a direct hit during an American four-engined bombing raid on the airfield at Pordenone/Oberitalien (east of the Po Basin).

The crews of the bombers usually consisted of a pilot, observer/navigator, radioman, mechanic and gunner. Together they formed a tightly knit team, and proved themselves to be up to the task in the Mediterranean and African theaters. With their successes, they earned the respect of the enemy. However, following the Allied landing in northwestern Africa, they began to suffer serious losses at the hands of the numerically and materially far superior Anglo-American air forces. The capitulation in Tunisia brought an end to the long and heroic operations of the bomber pilots in this theater.

In order to protect the German-Italian convoy routes from Italy to Africa and back, the Luftwaffe began a relentless series of attacks against Malta beginning during the first part of April 1942. A broad spectrum of Stukas, bombers, fighter-bombers, Zerstörers and fighters from various units took part in these attacks. The upper photo shows Stukas of StG 2 approaching their target, while the lower picture portrays an attack upon the harbor of La Valetta.

A Ju 88 of KG 77 over the harbor of La Valetta, preparing to make a bomb run on the La Venezia airfield.

This Ju 88 dropped its bombs on the harbor and canal works of La Valetta, leaving behind huge columns of smoke from the fires and explosions.

The grave of Staffelkapitän *Oblt.* Peter Riedinger, 3/StG 3, who was shot down by Hurricanes on 5 April 1942 between El Mechilis and Mfuts. His radioman, *Gefreiter* Heinz Wilke, also perished with him.

This photo, taken in April 1942 at Sicily's San Pietro airfield, shows a very fortunate pilot from 6/StG 2 (later 6/StG 3). *Lt.* Alex Heim brought his Ju 87 back safely after taking an anti-aircraft hit in the wing of his Stuka while on a mission over Malta. Heim's luck ran out on 1 February 1943 when he was shot down and killed by Kittyhawks following an attack on British tanks near Sened, Tunisia.

Left: **Bf 109s fly escort for Ju 87 B-2s. In spite of the noble efforts of the fighter pilots to protect their charges they were not able to prevent losses among the Stukas, which flew at a far slower speed.**

Right: **ground crewmen of II Gruppe of KG 26 seen loading a torpedo under an He 111. The Gruppe's He 111s had been fighting in the Mediterranean and North Africa since December 1940. In February 1941 the 6th Staffel was modified for torpedo bombing, and the entire Gruppe followed suit in April 1942.**

The Gruppe repeatedly enjoyed considerable success in spite of the protection of warships. This impressive photograph shows the results of an attack upon a freighter.

Characterized by an almost incomparable amount of assistance and compassion for both friend and foe alike, the pilots, doctors and teams of the Luftwaffe's medical units -especially those from the 1st Wüstennotstaffel — have found an enduring place in the history of the African conflict. The Staffelkapitän of the 1st Wüstennotstaffel, *Hptm.* Heinz Kroseberg (seen here in one of the last photos taken of him), was a role model for all. On May 12th 1942 the British shot down 9 fully loaded Ju 52 troop transports of TG 1 approximately 70km north of Derna. Flying his "Storch" (Stork) Kroseberg participated in the rescue efforts. He was observed throwing his own life preserver to the men struggling in the water; following that action, Kroseberg disappeared without a trace. The death of "Abu Markub" , the "Father of Storks" as he was known in Africa, was mourned by all, for many pilots had been saved from a certain death in the desert by Kroseberg. Heinz Kroseberg was posthumously awarded the Knight's Cross.

At the end of May 1942 Rommel once again moved on the offensive. The Stukas, as usual, were also involved. The aircraft, heavily loaded with bombs, take off from a field airstrip deep behind their own lines . . .

. . . make a low-level pass over the forward units of their own tank forces . . .

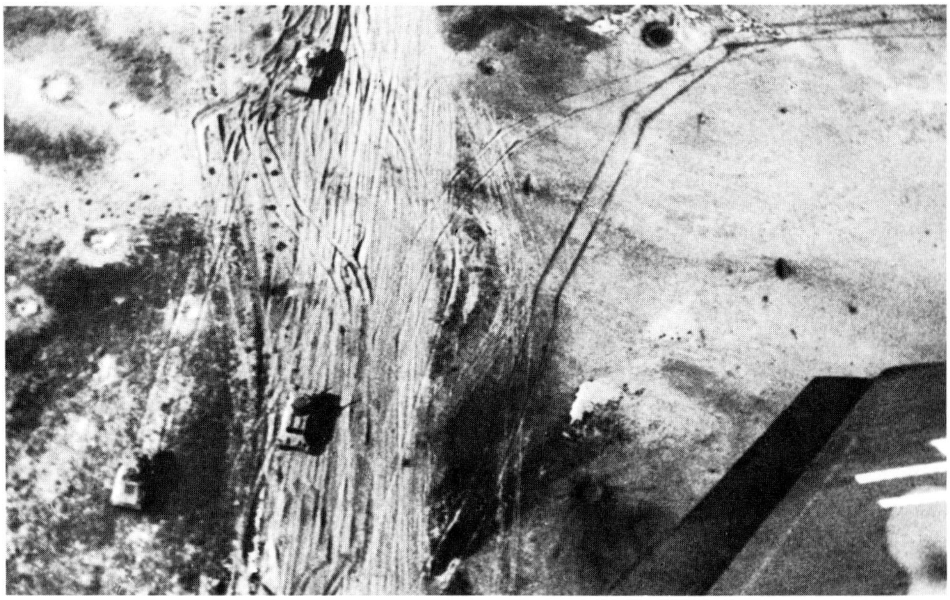

. . . and then fall upon the enemy's positions and tank units.

The enemy, too, makes use of all available aircraft to support its own ground troops and counter Rommel's offensive. Two Hurricane Is of 237 Squadron are seen here taking off.

Spitfire Mk V of the first Spitfire squadron (145 Squadron) to operate in North Africa. Gambut airfield in May 1942.

This Hurricane was captured by German troops in March 1941 during the British retreat, and was used for testing and courier service. Over a year later it fell into British hands again.

From May to October 1942 III/JG 53 "Pik As" fought with considerable success over North Africa. The photo shows a Rotte of Bf 109 F-2/Trop aircraft from this unit on a combat flight.

Hans-Joachim Marseille (here seated in his famous "Yellow 14") achieved his greatest successes during the many intense aerial battles of the spring and summer of 1942. These victories brought him the highest praise and honors, and at that time his name was mentioned in almost the same breath as Rommel's — by friend and foe alike.

His comrades also fought long and victoriously. *Lt.* Friedrich Körner (right) of 2/JG 27 observes the documentation of his fifth kill. After 36 victories in Africa he was shot down by the South African pilot *Lt.* Waugh and parachuted into imprisonment as a POW. There he received the Knight's Cross which had been awarded to him in absentia on 2 August 1942.

The Staffelkapitän's Ju 88 from the 1st Staffel of (Kampf-) Lehrgeschwader 1, parked at an airfield in North Africa. The aircraft on the left is a Ju 87 of StG 3.

The aircraft of LG 1 — here a Ju 88 of the 3rd Staffel — not only attacked targets in North Africa and on the sea, but also carried out repeated operations against La Valetta and other objectives on Malta.

A Ju 88 of 3/(Kampf-) Lehrgeschwader returns after a mission to Malta.

This aircraft of LG 1 made it all the way back to its home airfield after being shot up, only to be totally wrecked while making a belly landing.

During the summer of 1942 10/JG 27 (Jabostaffel, or fighter-bomber Staffel) also flew their Bf 109s from Sicily against Malta. Notice the thought-provoking message on the bomb, which reads: "Malta, Malta, you're disappearing, and with you goes all my fortune."

The desert airstrips looked the same in the enemy's camp as well. Only different types of aircraft were serviced there. This is a photograph of a Beaufighter from 252 or 272 Squadron.

Marylands of the South African Air Force taxi out for takeoff at a desert airstrip.

A Beaufort torpedo bomber, a dangerous opponent for the German-Italian shipping convoys.

Checking the guns at 9/ZG 26. The aircraft in the background is an Italian Savoia-Marchetti SM 79 bomber, which was also used with considerable success as a torpedo bomber by the Italians.

On 1 June 1942, the III/ZG 26 suffered a devastating loss. *Oblt.* Alfred Wehmeyer, commander of the 7th Staffel, was one of the best Zerstörer pilots in the Luftwaffe with 18 kills from over 200 combat flights. He was killed during a low-level attack west of Tobruk when his aircraft took a direct hit from an anti-aircraft shell. On 4 September 1942 he was posthumously awarded the Knight's Cross.

The end of a Bf 110 and its unfortunate crew. One of the engines malfunctioned on takeoff and the plane crashed and caught fire at the edge of the airfield.

Yet another photograph capturing the horrible reality of war: the burnt-out wreckage of a Hurricane which was shot down. The charred remains of the pilot are still in the wreckage.

With the horrors of combat staring them in the face each day, the soldiers made the best of it — given the circumstances. The slightest occasion was always an opportunity to celebrate. Here the 1st Staffel of an unidentified bomber unit rejoices at the completion of its 2000th combat mission.

Left: Ju 87s of StG 2 approaching a reported sighting of a British convoy. The bombs can clearly be seen underneath the fuselage and wings of the aircraft. ***Right:*** A cloudy evening sky frames two aircraft returning home after a successful mission.

This freighter was part of the great "Alexandria Convoy" when it was attacked and set on fire by Stukas on 14 June 1942, roughly 30km south of the island of Gardos.

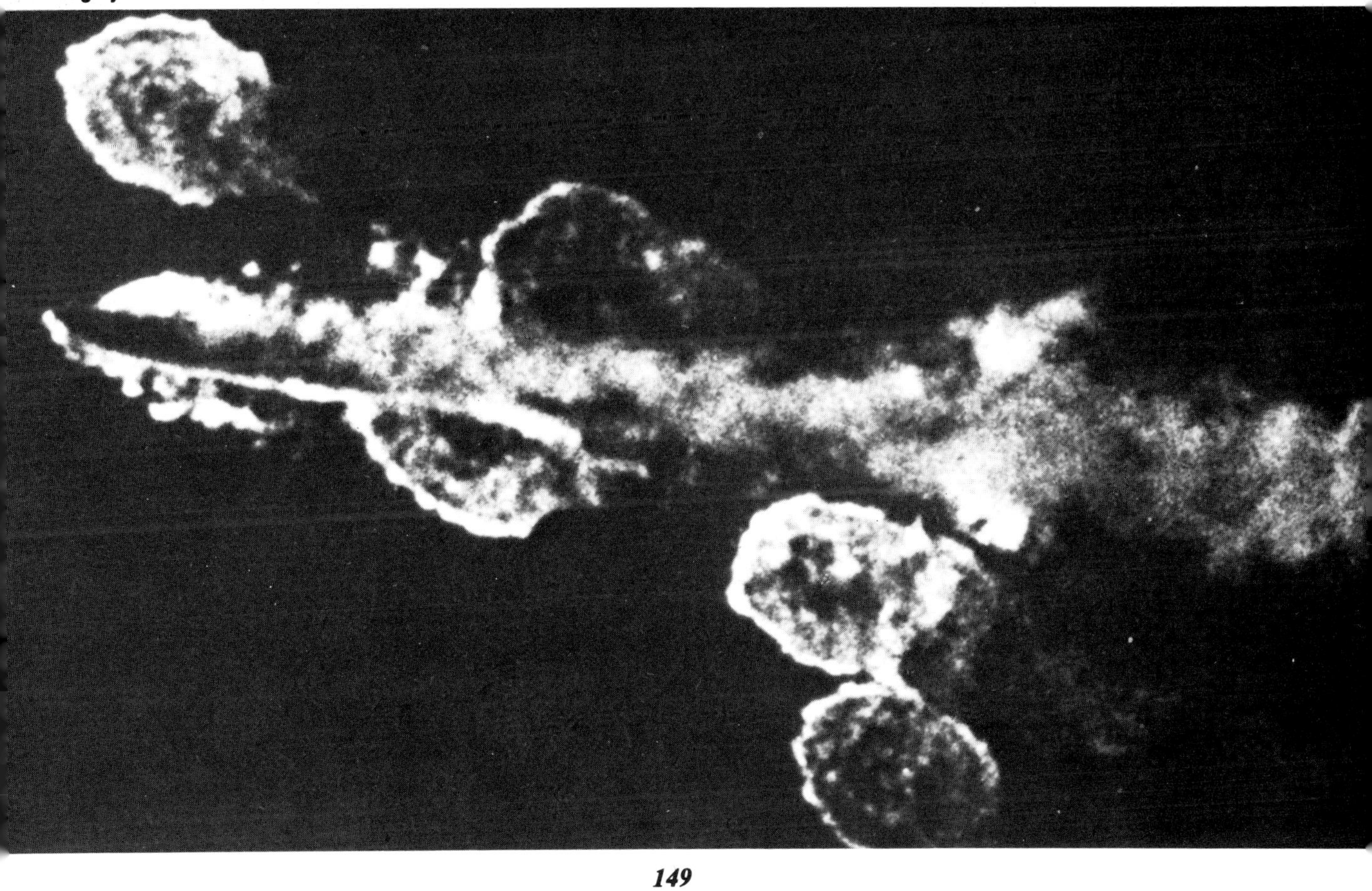

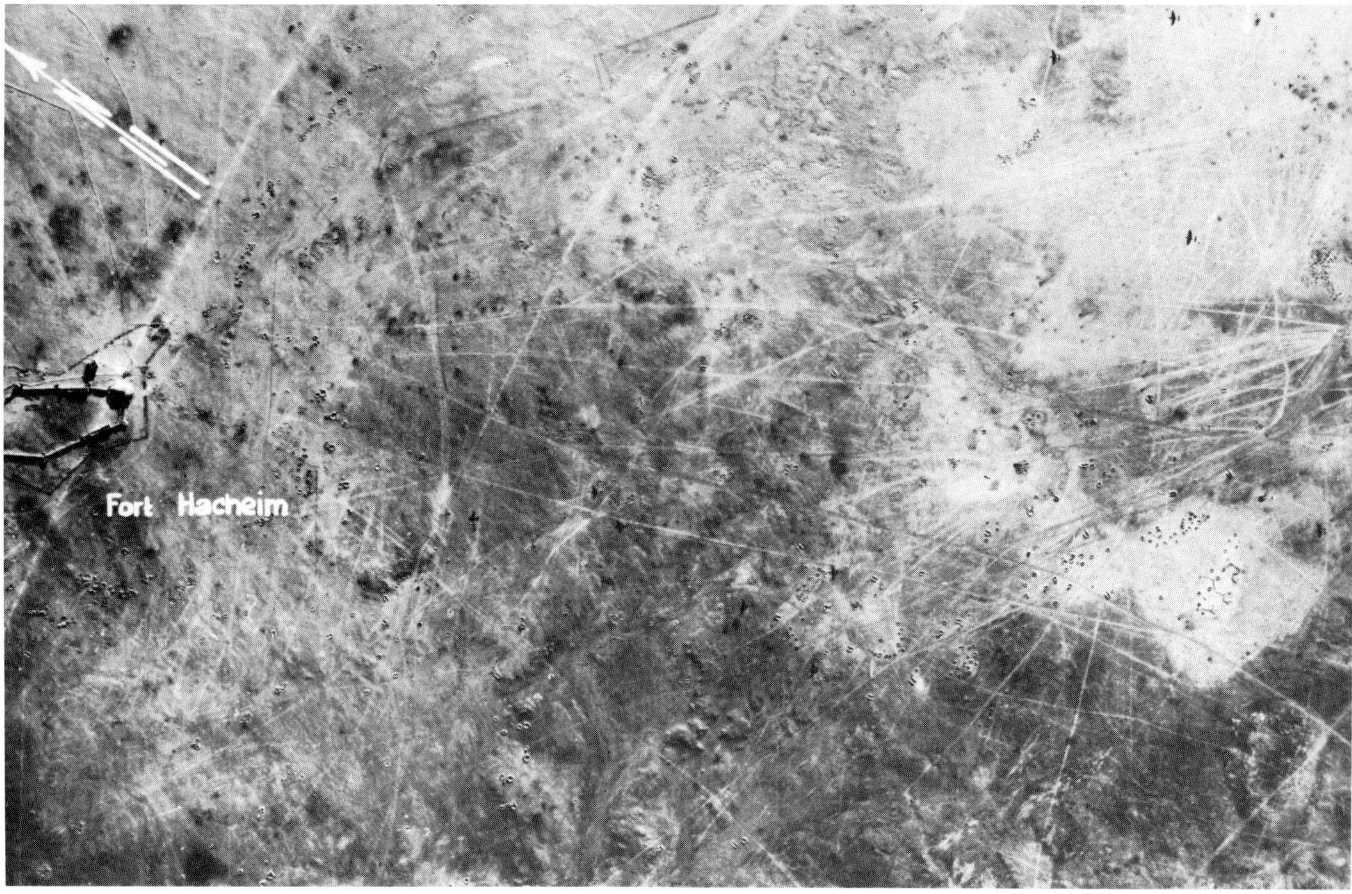

One of the rarest photographs of Luftwaffe operations to come out of the African campaign. Just before going into their diving attack, twelve Ju 87s of StG 3 can be seen approaching the British fort of Bir Hacheim. The fort was defended by the 1st Free French Brigade and a battalion of Jewish volunteers under the command of General Pierre Koenig. The 3000 French troops and 1000 members of the Jewish battalion put up the toughest resistance against Rommel and held on to the southernmost cornerstone of the Gazala front until 11 June 1942.

Fort Bir Hacheim and the surrounding area, seen caught in a hail of Stuka bombs.

The photographs of the attack on Fort Hacheim were taken by the crew of Felder/Muggenthaler from 1(F)/Aufkl. Gruppe 121.

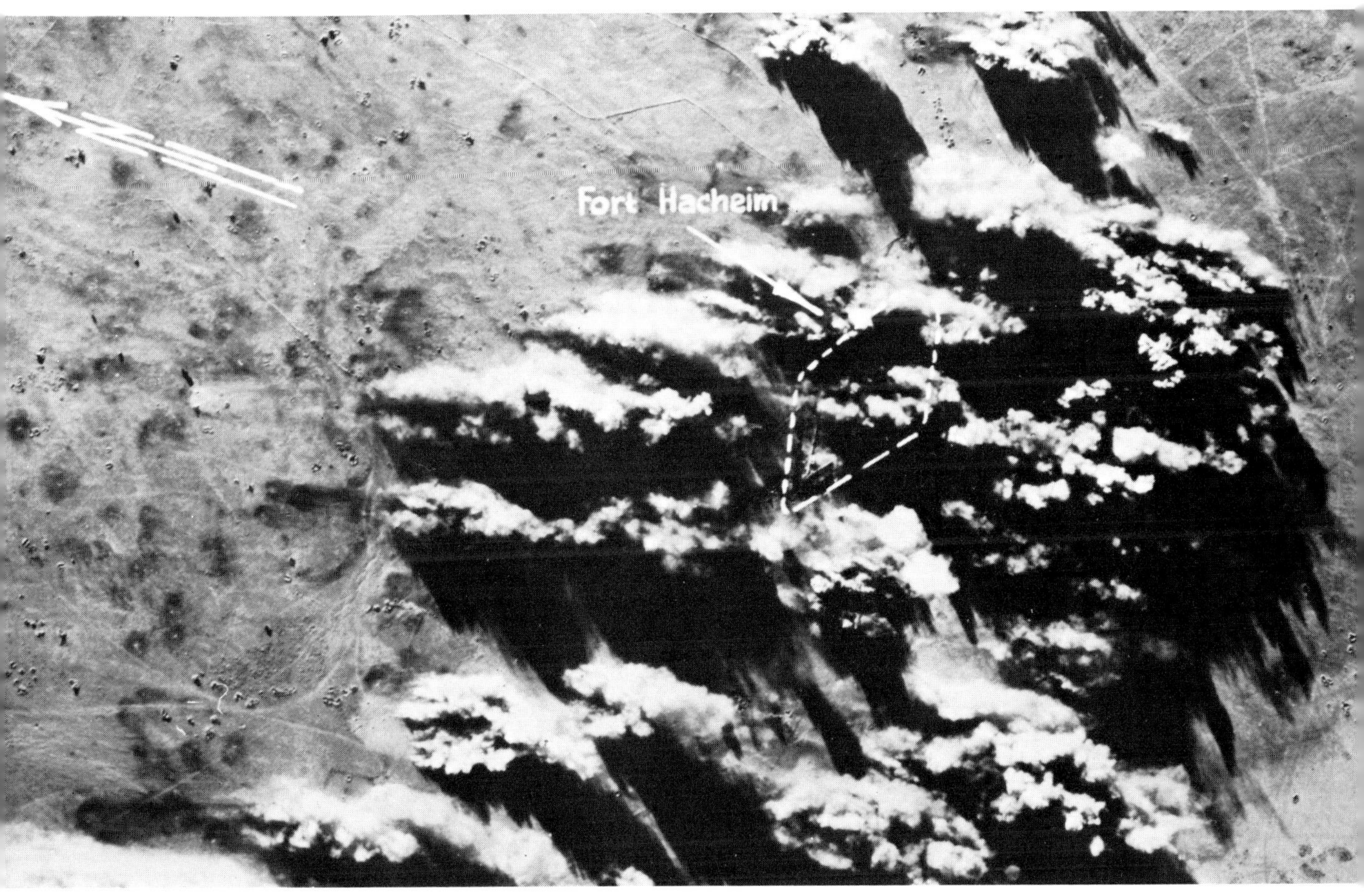

19 June 1942 at the El Adem airfield: Kesselring (center) is seen conversing with his officers. To the left is *Oberst* Alwin Wolz, commander of Flak-Rgt 135, one of the best commanders of the anti-aircraft artillery in Africa. Second from right is *Oblt.* Hans von Bargen of I/StG 3, counted among the most famous Stuka pilots in Africa.

The Stukas carried out repeated attacks on the freighters and warships in the harbor of Tobruk in an attempt to undermine the British supply efforts and bring Rommel closer to his goal of conquering Tobruk.

The Ju 88s of LG 1 also took part in the battles. The top picture shows aircraft of I Gruppe in between missions at the Derna airfield. *Below:* returning from a mission to Tobruk.

A Staffel of Ju 87s approaching British positions. Fighter protection is provided by a flight of Italian fighters.

German Stukas operating in the desert. (watercolor, painted 1941/1942).

Together with 12/(Kampf-)LG 1 and StG 3, the entire III/ZG 26 was placed under the command of *Oberstlt.* Sigel and took part in the DAK offensive. The ground crew fill the wing tanks of one of the Gruppe's Bf 110 . . .

. . . and lift a 250kg bomb under the fuselage.

The aircraft takes off for Tobruk, loaded with full tanks and two 250kg fuselage-mounted bombs and four 50kg wing-mounted bombs.

Wearer of the Knight's Cross *Hptm.* Christl (left), seen with a comrade taking a well-deserved rest between missions. As commander of III/ZG 26 from 25 December 1941 to 11 July 1943, Christl led the Gruppe with great success in both Africa and the Mediterranean area. The standard is the Geschwader insignia of ZG 26.

German tanks and motorized units of the DAK pass by a captured desert airfield. A Stuka from StG 2, apparently having belly-landed, lies next to the many destroyed British aircraft on the field. Souvenir hunters have cut the swastika from the aircraft's rudder.

After a brief but intense battle, Tobruk fell on 21 June 1942. This is what the city's harbor looked like to the German and Italian troops marching into the city.

Rommel continues to attack; this time his goal is the Nile. Operational conference with the "Fliegerführer Afrika", *Gen.Lt.* Hoffman von Waldau (second from left). Next to him, wearing the Knight's Cross, is *Hptm.* Redlich from JG 27. On the far right is *Major* i.G. Fuchs, the adjutant of the Fliegerführer Afrika.

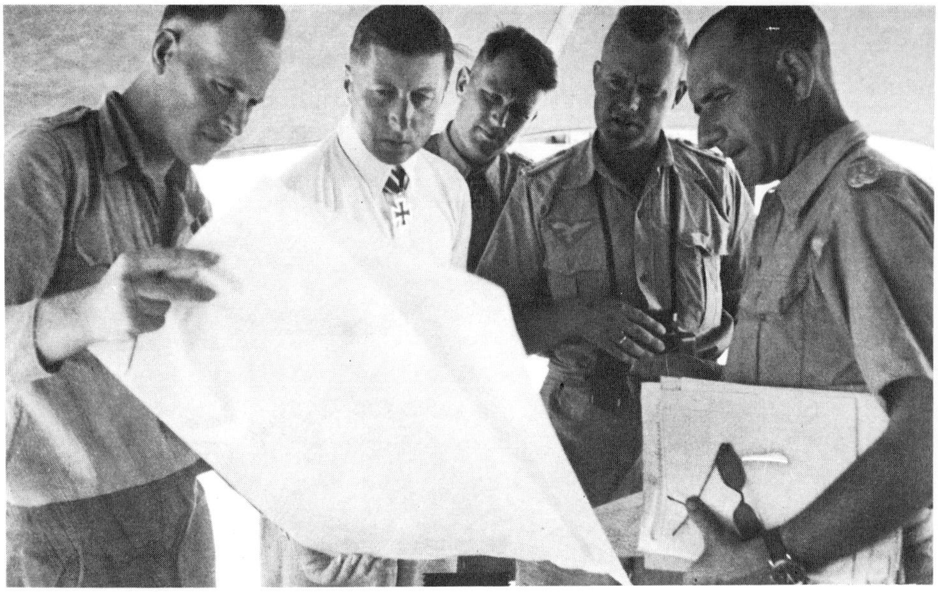

***Generalfeldmarschall* Kesselring was also constantly on the move and attempted to provide Rommel's tank army with all the protection and supplies possible by utilizing the Luftwaffe.**

Rommel — in the center, putting on his parachute — prepares to report back to Berlin. Fighter ace *Hptm.* Müncheberg is on the left and together with his men will be providing fighter protection on this flight. The He 111 (VG+ES) is the one used by Rommel as a transport aircraft.

The commander of II/StG 3, *Hptm.* Kurt Kuhlmey, was awarded the Knight's Cross on 15 July 1942 following 270 operational sorties. *Oberstlt.* Sigel, commander of StG 3, places the award around the neck of the "prince of El Hachin", as Kuhlmey was known among his friends.

General maintenance of a Ju 87 in the desert. The ground crew performed their work under unimaginably difficult conditions and played a decisive role in ensuring that the Luftwaffe remained capable of carrying out operations.

A "long range" wedding at III/ZG 26 on one of the airfields in Africa. The Gruppenkommandeur, *Hptm.* Christl, exercises his responsibilities as an official of the state.

Lt. Hans-Arnold Stahlschmidt, Staffelkapitän of 2/JG 27, scored 25 kills in July 1942 alone and was awarded the Knight's Cross on 20 August 1942. On 7 September 1942 he failed to return after a dogfight with Spitfires approximately 30km south of El Alamein, and was declared missing in action. During more than 400 missions in Africa — the highest number of combat sorties of all fighter pilots in the desert — he chalked up a total of 59 victories. On 3 January he was awarded the Oak Leaves to the Knight's Cross and promoted to *Oberleutnant* in absentia.

The commander of II/JG 27, *Major* Gustav Rödel (second from left), was one of the most successful fighter pilots in Africa with 52 kills (giving him a total of 98). He's seen here with his Staffel captains in front of the well-camouflaged, half-buried Gruppe's command post.

Yet another shot of the "blackmen", the ground crew, this time from I/JG 27. The aircraft which they're servicing in the scorching heat of Africa belongs to *Lt.* Stahlschmidt.

A game of Skat relieves some of the tension between the strenuous missions.

A Rotte of Ju 88s prepares to take off from an airfield on the island of Crete.

The famous "Helbig Flyers" (I/(Kampf-)LG 1) returning to Crete following an attack on the El Alamein positions. Since no enemy fighter activity is expected, the Ju 88s fly in a rather loose right echelon formation.

A great snapshot, taken from the cockpit of a Ju 88 looking forward toward the aircraft flying ahead.

July 1942 near Athens: *Generalmajor* Ramcke is seen here reviewing his paratrooper brigade shortly before its departure for North Africa. On the right is the battalion commander (later adjutant of the brigade) *Major* Kroh, who wears the Knight's Cross.

Dug into their positions around El Alamein, the paratroopers also became familiar with the difficulties of fighting in this combat theater. These troops were primarily used along the Ruweisat Ridge.

The brigade successfully took part in Rommel's final attack on the El Alamein positions, attacking limited targets. Under *Hptm.* Wiechmann, the brigade's artillery battalion provided outstanding support for the combatants.

At the beginning of September 1942 the British 132nd Tank Brigade attempted a breakthrough. Ramcke's paratroopers, together with their comrades in the Italian "Folgore" and "Trieste" Divisions, successfully repelled this attack.

The two lower photographs show *General* Ramcke and *Major* Kroh in conference with Italian officers, and (below) during an awards ceremony — presenting the Iron Cross Second Class to those soldiers of the previously named Italian units who proved themselves in the battle.

The African Stukas enjoyed another great victory on 14 September 1942. In a series of attacks off the coast of Tobruk they caught the British anti-aircraft cruiser "Coventry" and sank her. The lower picture shows the burning cruiser following the Stuka attack.

Escorted by Bf 110s of III/ZG 26, the "unnamed" but exceptionally heroic men of the transport units take off from Sicily and Crete once again to bring much-needed supplies to the Front across the Med.

29 September 1942 at the Kastelli airfield on Crete: *Ofw.* Helmut Haugk (second from left), one of the longest-serving Zerstörer pilots and member of III/ZG 26 has just returned from a patrol over the Mediterranean. On this mission he single-handedly intercepted a group of 11 B-24 Liberators, shot down two of them, and forced the rest to turn back. Representing all his fellow pilots, *Oblt.* Friedel Kowatsch, below, congratulates him on his victory with a cactus.

Hans-Joachim Marseille, the "Hunter of Africa", is dead! As this report went out over the ether, it sent out a wave of grief, dismay, and shock among the fighter pilots in Africa. Undefeated by the enemy, Marseille met a pilot's death on 30 September 1942 following a sortie. The engine of his new Bf 109 G-2/Trop, Werknr. 14256, "Yellow 14", suddenly cut out for no apparent reason and Marseille bailed out over his own lines near Sidi Abd El Rahman at 11:36am. He was knocked unconscious after striking the empennage and wasn't able to open his parachute before striking the ground.

He shot down 158 enemy aircraft on 388 combat missions, of which 151 kills were over the desert. The *General der Jagdflieger,* Adolf Galland, rightfully titled him as "the unrivaled virtuoso among the fighter pilots of the Second World War." Even today, the name of this brilliant fighter pilot — who was probably the most popular German soldier in Africa next to Rommel — lives on in the memories of friend and foe alike. The modern Bundesluftwaffe honored this outstanding pilot in October of 1977 by naming the barracks area of the Uetersen Airbase the "Marseille Kaserne."

With the new Macchi MC 202 the Regia Aeronautica finally was given an airplane which could produce good results. A flight of MC 202s is seen here patrolling the front.

Left page:
Two different roles for the Fi 156 "Storch." The picture above shows the aircraft used by *Generalfeldmarschall* Rommel and his entourage. The Stork below is being used to airlift a critically wounded DAK soldier. As elsewhere, the "Storch" was the most common all-purpose aircraft used by the Luftwaffe in Africa.

This Bf 109 F/Trop of the 7/JG 27 barely made it. After taking several hits the pilot managed to make a "smooth" belly landing in the desert.

In order to fulfill their varied missions the Zerstörer crews operated almost around the clock. This photo shows a Bf 110 with 300 liter metal drop tanks getting a last minute check before taking off on a new mission.

Italian merchant ships lie packed together in the harbor of Palermo, awaiting urgently needed supplies to carry to Africa.

Performing almost superhuman service in the African and Mediterranean theaters, without headlines or special reports, the transport pilots continually fulfilled their duty. Even in 1942, when their losses were tremendous.

A crew from III/KG zbV 1 stands in front of their Ju 52/3m transport, honored for having flown the 15000th sortie of the Gruppe.

Generalmajor Seidemann, since August 1942 the new "Fliegerführer Afrika", awards the Knight's Cross to (from left to right) Hans von Bargen and Herbert Stry and the German Cross in Gold to Fritz Eyer, Hubert Pölz and Alexander Heim, all from Stukageschwader 3. This ceremony took place on 5 October 1942 at Hagag el Qasaba in Egypt.

The 88mm anti-aircraft gun became a nightmare for the enemy in Africa. It was the single best weapon used against ground targets such as tanks, bunkers and artillery. This gun barrel displays a particularly successful weapon with 36 tank kills and 13 air kills.

This RAF Boston was severely damaged by flak and was forced to make an emergency landing behind German lines.

The German fighters fought a desperate battle against a numerically far superior foe on the Alamein front and during the retreat of the Heeresgruppe Afrika. A Bf 109 is seen landing at Fuka.

Swapping experience among the Experten during a break between missions (from left to right): *Oblt.* Keller, unknown, *Lt.* Schroer, who was awarded the Knight's Cross on 20 October 1942 after 49 victories, and *Lt.* Remmer, from 1 November 1942 the commander of 1/JG 27 (killed on 2 April 1944 during the defense of the Reich and posthumously awarded the Knight's Cross on 30 June 1944).

On 27 October 1942, the I/JG 27 arrived in Africa. Along with the Geschwader's other Gruppen, it was sent in order to relieve the other Jagdgruppen of JG 27 and III/JG 53 which were gradually rotating out of the theater. On the left is the Staffelkapitän of 2/JG 27, Wearer of the Knight's Cross Siegfried Freytag, with his comrades after landing. The aircraft in the background is the "Black 1" of the Staffelkapitän.

The tactical reconnaissance units provided exceptional quality results in the African theater. One member of these units was *Leutnant* Ludwig Hammer, pilot and observer of 2(H)/14, the Aufklärungsstaffel of the Deutsche Afrikakorps, later transferred to Aufkl. Gruppe 4(H)/12.

The photo shows *Lt.* Hammer after returning from a sortie in his Bf 109 F. He was one of the tactical reconnaissance pilots who provided invaluable service during the Battle for El Alamein and during the November 1942 retreat of the Panzerarmee Afrika. For his performance he was awarded the German Cross in Gold, and on 29 October 1943, after nearly 700 combat sorties (over 500 in Africa alone) he was presented the Knight's Cross.

A Ju 88 of the Aufklärungsstaffel of Lehrgeschwader 1 flies an armed reconnaissance patrol over the eastern Med. Notice that the aircraft is only flying on its right engine.

The bomber pilots also made repeated attempts to relieve their Army comrades by carrying out attacks of all types. This is a Ju 88 from the feared "Helbig Flyers" (I Gruppe of (Kampf-)LG 1), seen prior to taking off on a mission over the sea.

This is an aircraft of the 4th Staffel of (Kampf-)LG 1, L1+IM, loaded with bombs on a combat flight.

On 10 September 1942 the former KüFlgGr 606 was incorporated into KG 77 as I/KG 77. This Gruppe enjoyed considerable success against naval targets, but flew missions into North Africa as well. This is a Ju 88 A-4 of this unit.

On 8 November 1942, 3Z+DB, a Ju 88 A (Werknr. 1016) of the Headquarters unit of I/KG 77, is greeted by comrades as it returns from a combat sortie.

The occasion for this joyous celebration was the 100th combat mission of *Uffz.* August Seemann. On his left is his pilot, *Lt.* Johannes Geismann, who was awarded the Knight's Cross for sinking a ship on 21 December 1942. The Ju 88's rudder in the background shows the official tally for the Geismann crew.

Operations of Fallschirmjäger-Brigade Ramcke in Africa

After the return of the partially decimated paratrooper (Fallschirmjäger) forces from Russia, *General der Flieger* Student rebuilt his elite troops from scratch in the spring of 1942. Together with *Generalmajor* Ramcke, one of the best generals of the Fallschirm-truppe (who was still a parachutist at the age of 51!), Student worked on a plan at the request of Kesselring for the capture of the island fortress of Malta. This undertaking was to be performed by the combined German and Italian paratrooper and airborne forces, supported by the air force's flying units from both countries. The plan called for the Italian fleet, with all its ships (including its battle-ships), to provide for sea transport and safety. The operation was to be carried out under the direction of the Italian Comando Supremo lcd by Colonel General Graf Cavallero. Hitler, however, had serious doubts about the reliability of his Axis partner and, after some hesitation, finally cancelled "Unter-nehmen Herkules." This was a decision which could have had an entirely different effect on the prosecution of the war in the Mediterranean and Africa.

The paratroopers were therefore freed up for other uses, and Ramcke received the assignment to equip a brigade and fly to Africa in order to beef up Rommel's Panzer-armee. By and by a 2000 man brigade was formed near Athens, consisting of four rifle battalions, an artillery division, and one company each of armored rifle and engineers. At the end of July/beginning of August 1942 they were transferred by way of Crete to Tobruk. Other than a few motorcycles, the unit had no vehicles, and the soldiers were forced to "hitchhike" aboard various trans-ports in order to reach their end destination — the Alamein position. There, primarily used along the Ruweisat Ridge, they learned through harsh static warfare the difficulties of this theater. On the 30th of August 1942 Rommel renewed his attacks. After intense fighting, the Brigade Ramcke finally reached its target of Deir el Munassib.

The paratroopers dug in here, and suc-cessfully warded off all attacks by the 132nd British Armored Brigade. Its commander, Major-General Clifton, and 350 of his men were taken prisoner; Ramcke's brigade also destroyed 16 tanks and 80 troop, weapons, and reconnaissance vehicles. This notable success was reported by the brigade on 4 September. Their Italian paratrooper comrades, who fought exceptionally well, also played a role in this victory.

On 23 October 1942, the British 8th Army, under its new supreme commander Mont-gomery, launched a massive counteroffensive under the protective umbrella of total air superiority. This attack was launched fol-lowing several hours of artillery bombard-ment and air strikes. However, the British only conducted feinting attacks in Ramcke's sector, for the primary objective of the offensive lay to the north, in the coastal area.

During the evening of 2 November, the brigade received orders to disengage from the enemy and assume new positions. Not having any form of motorized transport available, the soldiers were forced to make a night march of 30 kilometers under the most difficult conditions. On the evening of 3 November, after only one day in their new position, the unit was instructed to deploy a battalion to the north. In order to carry out these new orders this battalion received nearly all of the brigade's vehicles, and *Hptm.* Straehler-Pohl began the march to the north with 40 cargo transports. This column had hardly disappeared in the distance when the entire brigade was ordered to move out, for they were now in danger of being cut off and destroyed. The brigade was to assume a new position west of Fuka, which meant a four-day 100km march through the desert.

Now almost completely without vehicles — only the artillery and motorized rifle units were transported out of necessity — the brigade marched westward, hard-pressed by the British both day and night. During the night of 5/6 November they fell upon a British transport column. The paratroopers overpowered the crew in hand-to-hand fighting and confiscated the vehicles. As it turned out, they were part of a British tank unit and contained everything that Ramcke's men needed. Following their 350km-long adventurous retreat through the desert, they finally came upon the coastal highway west of Mersa Matruh. The brigade stumbled upon a German reconnaissance division and were rescued. A short time later Ramcke reported to Rommel, who had given the brigade up for lost, with the words "He leevet noch!" (We're still alive!). On 16 November 1942, Bernhard Ramcke was awarded the Oak Leaves to the Knight's Cross of the Iron Cross.

Following this retreat, the majority of the brigade was transferred back to Germany. Under the leadership of *Major* Freiherr von der Heydte (Wearer of the Knight's Cross) one battalion was brought up to the strength of a Kampfgruppe. This unit was used as a rear guard, continuing to fight as Rommel retreated westward, and saw action in Tunisia up until the end in May of 1943.

One of the unforgotten feats of the German Luftwaffe during the Second World War was the 350km retreat foot march by the Fallschirmbrigade Ramcke in November 1942 following the battle of El Alamein — only the artillery and armored infantry troops were transported out of necessity. Ramcke, together with his men, reported back to Rommel on November 7th with the words "Ne leevet noch!" ("We're still alive!").

This, too, was Africa! Poisonous scorpions and sand vipers (the largest poisonous snake in Central Europe and one of North Africa's most dangerous), as well as the harmless desert lizard were some of the local denizens.

Troops of the anti-aircraft artillery units also enjoyed considerable success in Africa during 1942, especially in combat against tanks. In particularly threatening situations these men had even been known to keep the front lines from collapsing.

Uffz. Emil Berner, gunner of the 3/FlakRgt 18, was awarded the Knight's Cross on 12 November 1942 while in the rank of *Gefreiter* for destroying no less than 42 tanks in North Africa.

Wachtmeister Reinhard Melzer (right) with a comrade, standing in front of a British Mathilda Mk II tank which he destroyed. Melzer had already been awarded the Knight's Cross a year previously for his victories in the Battle of Sollum.

Oblt. Franz Schweiger (right), who's not even letting the photographer disturb his lunch, received the high honor on 14 February 1942 while commander of the 8/FlakRgt 25. Up to that time his battery had knocked out 43 enemy tanks in Africa. When one of his gunners was hit, he personally jumped in as the replacement on the gun and destroyed 16 of the attacking tanks.

Flak gunners seen performing minor maintenance on their 88mm gun, which sits in a position to counter tank attacks and has makeshift protection against shell fragments. The next gun of the battery can be seen in the distance.

Left: On 8 November 1942, the Allies landed in Northwest Africa. One day later *Oberst* Harlinghausen was named as "Fliegerführer Tunesien" and on the same day landed at the El Aouina airfield outside of Tunis. For his outstanding leadership he was promoted to *Generalmajor* on 1 December 1942. From left to right: Theo Osterkamp ("Jafü", or Commander of Fighter Forces in Italy), Harlinghausen, and an unknown person.

Right: On 22 January 1943, *Generalmajor* Seidemann replaced Harlinghausen, who took command of II Fliegerkorps, as the "Fliegerführer Tunesien." Seidemann, who since 1 August 1942 was already functioning as "Fliegerführer Afrika", was named as Commanding General of the Fliegerkorps Tunis on 1 February 1943.

Hptm. Wilhelm Hachfeld, Wearer of the Knight's Cross and commander of III/ZG 26 collided with a landing aircraft as he was attempting to take off in Bizerta on 2 December 1942. His aircraft flipped over and the bomb it was carrying exploded. He had earned the knickname "Bomben-Willi" for his efforts to develop a fighter-bomber branch of the service. On 650 combat sorties, of which 230 were fighter-bomber operations, Hachfeld scored 11 aerial victories and destroyed 32 ground targets. Once again, the German Luftwaffe had lost one of its finest.

I Gruppe of the newly formed SchG 2 was deployed to North Africa in November 1942 to support the defensive battles and assist in protecting retreating friendly forces. The Gruppe flew the new Hs 129 B attack aircraft, which had already proved its worth in Russia.

An Hs 129 B of the 4/(Panzer-)SchG 2 is made ready for takeoff while a formation of Ju 52 transports lands in the Background.

A Rotte of Hs 129 B aircraft from the Panzerjägerstaffel of I/SchG 2 takes off. This unit also proved effective in North Africa and Tunisia.

On 18 December 1942, *Feldwebel* Anton Hafner (Wearer of the Knight's Cross) of II/JG 51 "Mölders", shot down a P-38 Lighting on the outskirts of Tunis. The pilot, Lt. Norman Widen, was able to bail out and landed close to the wreckage of his aircraft near the German airfield. The center picture shows "Toni" Hafner and his comrades talking with Lt. Widen (in leather jacket). His eyes are smeared black to protect against the glare of the bright sun. 19 years later the brother of "Toni" Hafner, who was killed on 17 October 1944 in East Prussia after his 204th victory, welcomed the former American fighter pilot back to Germany and presented him with a few memoirs of the dead fighter pilot. A gesture of friendship and reconciliation between former enemies.

Hptm. Bernhard Hamester, from 31 December 1942 commander of III/StG 3, was one of the most famous Stuka "aces" in North Africa. He was fortunate to leave Africa after over 400 combat missions, but fate caught up with him during the final battles for the defense of the homeland. Then a *Major* and Kommodore of StG 3, he was shot down and killed on 22 April 1945 while making a low-level attack against Stalin tanks.

In spite of the great danger and high losses at the hands of Allied fighters and anti-aircraft, several Stuka units continued to fly up until the bitter end in May 1943 as a sort of "fire department" for the ground forces in North Africa and Tunisia.

The ground crew work at a high pace at the jump-off points in Italy, getting the Ju 52s ready for the emergency airlift to Tunisia. The aircraft themselves have been commandeered from a variety of units.

While the ground and air crew get the planes ready, their "passengers" — with tropical gear and their weapons — are already waiting at the airfield.

The Ju 52/3m transports seen on the dangerous journey across the Mediterranean in the direction of Tunis. Above the fuselage, the gunners can be clearly seen manning their MG 15 machine guns.

After their arrival, a united effort is made to pull a motorcycle with sidecar out of the loading hatch. On the upper fuselage can be seen the MG 15 gun and plexiglass windscreen, which also acts as a deflector for the gun. The gunner, wearing a life preserver, remains at his post for the present.

A view of a Ju 52/3m being refueled (notice the rather odd fuel pump). This aircraft carries a so-called "Condor-Haube DL 15A" plexiglass windscreen for the forward MG 15 position above the cockpit.

Indian prisoners of war were used to build airfields, assist in loading and unloading the transports, and for other tasks.

Operations of the Paratroopers and the "Hermann Göring" Division in Tunisia

Under the command of General Eisenhower, 107,000 Allied soldiers began landing in Casablanca, Oran and Algiers on 8 November 1942. However, since the Allied forces had been unable to capture the harbors and airfields at Tunis and Bizerta, the Oberbefehlshaber Süd *Generalfeldmarschall* Kesselring was able to react quickly. The situation required a bridgehead in Tunisia. This assignment was entrusted to Nehring, *General der Panzertruppen* (General of Panzer Troops).

On 9 November, the newly named "Fliegerführer Tunesien", *Oberst* Harlinghausen, was the first to land. His airplane, an He 111 accompanied by a few Ju 52s and aircraft from JG 53, touched down at the El Aouina airfield outside of Tunis. At the time, El Aouina was occupied by the French, who decided to remain neutral. This made it possible for a paratrooper company under the command of *Hptm.* Sauer to land there one day later. Sauer's company was initially utilized to provide security for the following landings of the paratrooper and army units at the two airfields in Tunis — La Marsa and El Aouina. By and by the first small groups of troops arrived, among them a company of the Wachbataillon (Guards Battalion) of *Feldmarschall* Kesselring and a paratrooper engineering platoon under *Feldwebel* Peter Arent. At the beginning of December *Feldwebel* Arent distinguished himself in a battle for the bridge at El Bathan, an action for which he received the Knight's Cross. Unfortunately, he was killed in action on 4 December 1942.

On 11 November an advance party of FJR 5 (Fallschirmjäger-Regiment 5, or Paratrooper Regiment 5) arrived, and by the 15th the regiment was up to its full strength of two battalions under the command of *Oberstlt.* Koch. The first large-scale conflict between German and American forces occurred on 19-20 November at Medjez el Bab, when FJR 5 and the 1st U.S. Armored Division found themselves facing each other. By the end of November the so-called Luftwaffe-Regiment Barenthin had arrived in Tunis with the Fallschirm-Korps-Pionier-Batl. 21 under Major Witzig, along with significant numbers from the 10th Panzer Division and the Schwere Panzer-Tiger-Abt. 501 (Heavy Panzer, Tiger Battalion 501). By using these resources, *General* Nehring was able to construct a front and secure it at the his victorious Battle of Tebourba (1-4 December 1942). The paratrooper units performed in an outstanding manner during this engagement, which ensured that the "Race for Tunis" was won.

As the six-month struggle for the Tunisian Bridgehead continued, the paratroopers (consisting of FJR 5, now with three battalions and incorporated into the "HG" Division on 14 Mar, the LW-Rgt Barenthin, and the Fs.Pi.Batl.) fought hard in all the hot spots along the front, losing many of their number. Numerous older, battle-tested paratroopers lost their lives here during this period. The losses suffered among the officer and NCO ranks was especially high.

In order to strengthen the bridgehead, it was decided to send in the "Hermann Göring" Division, which was first organized in southern France. The first "HG" units arrived in Africa in December of 1942. In January 1943 the fully-equipped Flak-Rgt.

under *Oberstlt.* Hullmann with two battalions was brought over by ship. As a rule, the transport of the "HG" units to Tunisia took place by air from Naples and Trapani — without their heavy equipment, however. This equipment was to be brought in by sea, but often arrived too late or not at all. These problems naturally had a strong influence on the units' operational readiness and their combat strength.

The division received valuable reinforcements with the incorporation of FJR 5, which was officially given the new designation of Jägerregiment (Rifle Regiment) "HG" on 14 March 1943. The deployment of the full division to Africa was postponed until April and was cancelled altogether on 19 April, when it was obvious that the end of the bridgehead was rapidly approaching. Therefore, only individual units of the "HG" Division took part in the fighting in Tunisia. The highest troop strength reached by the division in Tunisia was roughly 11,000 men. *Oberst* — from April on *Generalmajor* — Josef Schmid (called "Beppo"), who arrived in Africa during New Year's, commanded the units. These units were initially referred to as "Kampfgruppe Schmid", and in Tunisia only officially received the designation "HG" Division beginning in April.

In spite of their inferior numbers and the absolute air superiority of the Allies, the fighting spirit and resolve of the German troops — and a few of the Italian elite units — remained unbroken. The members of the "HG" Division, too, fought bitterly until the last day, fulfilling their military duty by remaining at their posts — even in hopeless situations. They distinguished themselves bravely during Operation "Fliederblüte", a thrust into the enemy's staging area on 20 April near the division's northern sector, and during the defense of the hills southeast of Medjez el Bab (such as Hill 107, the "Cactus Farm").

As with all German units, 13 May saw an end to combat in Tunisia for the remainder of the "HG" Division, too; only a few of the survivors managed to escape an imprisonment lasting up to several years. The division was never able to fully recover from this blood-letting, despite its later reorganization. In Tunisia it had lost many of those who had joined from the Landespolizei in 1935 to form the "General Göring" Regiment, as well as many volunteers who enlisted beginning in 1936 — all well-trained and battle-hardened soldiers.

Left behind were the division's dead, who now rest in the soldier's cemetery at Bordj Cedria — a warning to those now living and future generations of our responsibility to direct our efforts toward the preservation and protection of peace.

The German paratroopers are here! The soldiers march through Tunis, astounded and sometimes even joyfully welcomed by the local populace.

Initially, only observation and reconnaissance activities are undertaken in this rough and often intraversible landscape. Sometimes, though, the local inhabitants provide assistance.

Initial positions are taken up, and the paratroopers — here manning an sMG 42 — also give their all in the Tunisian theater under great sacrifice.

Highly-decorated commanders who have proven themselves on every battlefield lead the men of FJR 5 (later FJR "HG") in Tunisia. From left to right: *Hptm.* Jungwirt, *Oberstlt.* Koch, the regiment's commander, *Oblt.* Hoefeld and *Major* Schirmer.

Although without any heavy weapons, the troops wait for the enemy's onslaught with the most modern light weapons (here the LIG 75 — a 75mm light infantry gun with a range of 3 to 4 kilometers).

The excellent light infantry gun seen firing.

During tough fighting the soldiers achieve their first victories in Tunisia. Natives are curiously inspecting an enemy tank knocked out at close range and look in awe at a heavily-armed German paratrooper.

Earned during the fighting in Tunisia, the first decorations are given out. Wearer of the Knight's Cross *Major* Witzig, commander of the Fallschirm-Pionier-Bataillon, hands out the awards.

But there weren't only the victories. There were also many painful and bitter losses. Among these was *Oblt.* Erich Schuster, beloved by all soldiers and awarded the Knight's Cross while still a *Feldwebel* on 21 August 1941 for his efforts in securing the Malemes Airfield on Crete. The commander of 1/FJR 5 (1./FJR "HG") was killed on 11 January 1943 and laid to rest on the 13th in the La Mornaghia cemetery.

Left: Generalmajor Gottlob Müller, commanding general and chief of the Tunis Luftgau (air district), played a major role in the operations and victories of the Luftwaffe units in Tunisia fighting a hopeless battle against overwhelming odds. As with so many others, this highly effective Luftwaffe general lost his life in the Battle of Berlin, on 20 April 1945.

Right: Generalfeldmarschall Kesselring (center) and *Generalmajor* Buchholz (left), the commander of air transport in Tunisia, are greeted by *Generaloberst* von Arnim shortly after landing in Tunis. Von Arnim was the last commander-in-chief of the German-Italian Heeresgruppe Afrika.

The Do 215 B-1 used by *Generalfeldmarschall* Kesselring as a transport aircraft. Below the pilot's cockpit is the insignia of Luftflotte II, the Luftwaffe eagle with crossed marshal's standards and the number 2 on a shield.

Operating from Trapani, Sicily, the new Messerschmitt 210 fighter joined in the fight. The pilots, however, had little luck or success with this aircraft, which was eagerly anticipated as a multi-role aircraft. Apparently of a poor design, the aircraft didn't live up to expectations and was taken out of combat operations. These photos show aircraft from Versuchsstaffel 210 (Test Staffel 210), which markings can be seen in the white fuselage band on the aircraft in the upper photo. The white band was the identification for those aircraft operating in the Mediterranean area and North Africa.

After the Americans had landed on the Moroccan coast, KG 30 ("Adler-Geschwader") was moved from the far north down to Comiso. This Geschwader had operated with considerable effectiveness in the anti-shipping role. Under the leadership of their commander, Werner Baumbach (Wearer of the Swords to the Knight's Cross and one of the best bomber pilots in the Luftwaffe), the Geschwader conducted costly operations against the Allied supply routes off the North African coast and its harbors.

Major Baumbach awards the Knight's Cross to *Oblt.* Helmut Weinrauch, commander of III/KG 30, on 22 January 1943. Baumbach was killed in a plane crash on 20 October 1950 in Argentina, and Weinrauch fell during the defense of the Reich on 18 November 1943 while flying an Fw 190. At the time of his death he had been promoted to *Oberstleutnant* and was commander of JG 301.

One of the heavy bombs used to carry out attacks against the Allies' ships and harbor facilities.

The Luftwaffe's leadership took great pains to strengthen the fighter defense in Tunisia. Bf 109s with the external fuel tanks for the long flight were transferred from the homeland and are seen landing in Tunisia after brief stops in Italy and Sicily.

One of the "new ones" was the fighter ace *Oblt.* Fritz Dinger (who was awarded the Knight's Cross for 49 victories and over 500 combat sorties). Here the commander of 4/JG 53 "Pik As" makes first contact with the "real" Africans.

During the breaks between missions the soldiers use the time to grab a quick bite from their field kitchens. This is a snapshot taken at III/JG 77.

The enemy, too, made use of all available aircraft in an attempt to bring the war in Africa to a quick and victorious close. Here Wellington night bombers of 205 Group are seen taking off from a desert strip.

This photo was taken during an overflight of a Baltimore bomber.

The air superiority of the Allies was great and had a direct impact upon the losses suffered by the Germans and Italians in both men and material. Again and again, this is what the majority of German airfields looked like following a bomber raid or low-level attack.

The Italian fighters — here a Macchi MC 202 — gave their best during heroic and often costly operations in Tunisia.

Long range reconnaissance aircraft observed the supply convoys and landing operations of the Allies. They also provided the necessary data to support attacks by the German bomber units. This picture shows a Ju 88 A-10 of 2/AufklGr (F) 123.

Generalfeldmarschall **Rommel pays a visit to his successful reconnaissance pilots in Tunisia. The man on the right is** ***Hptm.*** **Erwin Fischer, commander of 1/(F) 121.**

A momentous occasion for *Hptm.* Erwin Fischer and his crew, who've just completed the 3000th operational sortie by the 1st Staffel of Fernaufklärungs-Gruppe 121. A few days later, on 8 February 1943, Fischer was the first reconnaissance pilot in the Luftwaffe to be awarded the Oak Leaves to the Knight's Cross. He had flown 273 operational combat sorties. This award not only spoke for his personal abilities, but also provided recognition and honor for all the reconnaissance crews operating in Africa and the Mediterranean.

In spite of the superiority of the British and American air forces in Tunisia, the Stukas continued to fly effective missions in support of their comrades in the army and the paratroopers. Their effectiveness, however, was all too often bought at the price of heavy losses.

Ju 87 D-3, S7+FR of 7/StG 3, is seen returning from a mission in Gabut-West in February 1943.

On 6 February 1943, the III/ZG 26 had reason to celebrate when a crew of the 9th Staffel completed the 10000th sortie. On the left is the Gruppe's commander, *Hptm.* Christl, and on the right is *Ofw.* Haugk. Unfortunately, the names of the two flyers being celebrated are not known.

Yet another noteworthy occasion for this famous Zerstörer Gruppe was when King Victor Emanuel III paid a visit in Trapani Sicily. The picture shows the king standing in the car as he and his entourage prepare to leave. The Gruppenkommandeur, Wearer of the Knight's Cross *Hptm.* Georg Christl, is seen walking next to the car.

The Hs 129 armored ground attack aircraft enjoyed considerable success as well. It was nicknamed the "Flying Can Opener" by pilots and ground troops alike.

***Oblt.* Oswald, commander of 8/(Pz)SchG 2, awards five of his pilots with the Iron Cross Second Class for their operations with the Henschel Hs 129. From left to right: *Lt.* Junck, *Uffz.* Lebanz, *Oblt.* Oswald, *Uffz.* Krause, unknown *Feldwebel,* and *Lt.* Petz.**

Oblt. **Oswald and his comrades inspect a captured American General Lee tank. After 50 tank kills and over 300 missions in the Hs 129, Oswald was awarded the Knight's Cross on 24 October 1944 while a *Hauptmann*.**

The "Flying Tank Killers" not only were effective against their main enemy the tank, but also during low level attacks against positions, supply routes and airfields — as these pictures demonstrate.

These operations were not flown without their losses, however. An Hs 129 B of 8/(Pz)SchG 2 was fortunately able to make a crash landing.

While the mechanics of the recovery team take out the aircraft's guns, Arabs are deep in discussion at the crash site. Even a noble tribal brother, mounted on his horse, has taken it upon himself to view the fallen bird.

Ju 52/3m transports at the Castel Vetrano, which together with Trapani was one of the most utilized jump-off points for supply operations to Tunisia.

These transports have almost made it. Flying in a somewhat loose formation, they come in for a landing. The remains of numerous Ju 52s destroyed in Allied fighter-bomber raids can be seen in the foreground.

Ju 52/3m transports landing at an airfield in Tunisia. Along with the constant threat from the air, landings and takeoffs placed the greatest demands upon the transport crews.

During the airlift in support of the Tunisian Bridgehead the Me 323 "Gigant" (Giant) also proved to be most effective. The aircraft had six French Gnome et Rhône M 14 engines and could lift over 22 tons into the air. The pictures show Me 323 Ds of II/TG 5 with their Gruppe's insignia, which was applied to both sides of the aircraft below the cockpit.

Having just landed in their transport aircraft, members of the "Hermann Göring" Division keenly observe the Messerschmitt fighters of III/JG 53 "Pik As" taking off.

In the skies over Tunisia, the Focke-Wulf Fw 190 single-seat fighter was seen for the first time in the African theater. This new fighter was on par with, and even often superior to its foe. In air combat and as a fighter-bomber, the Fw 190 enjoyed considerable success. This shows an Fw 190 flying over a burning tank it had destroyed with its internal guns.

One of the greatest fighter aces in Tunisia was *Lt.* Kurt Bühligen, a Wearer of the Knight's Cross from II/JG 2 "Richthofen." Bühligen, who had come from the Channel front, shot down 40 British and American aircraft from December 1942 to March 1943. By the end of the war his tally stood at 112 kills, among them 14 four-engine bombers, and he had gone from *Gefreiter* to *Oberstleutnant* and commander of the reputable JG 2 "Richthofen."

The Zerstörer pilots continued their uninterrupted fighting against a superior enemy. In spite of the strain of operations, this crew (*Uffz.* Helmut Zittier and *Uffz.* Walter Stolz) from 7/ZG 26 poses cheerfully in front of their Bf 110 at the Sousse airfield.

Once again, it's time to bid farewell to a great German fighter pilot. On 23 March 1943, the commander of JG 77, *Major* Joachim Müncheberg, was killed on his 500th mission in a dogfight with Spitfires southwest of Maknassy. He plummeted to his death when the wings of his aircraft came off. Müncheberg had achieved a total of 135 victories, 33 of them in Russia, and wore the Knight's Cross with Oak Leaves and Swords. In addition, he was also awarded the Italian Golden Medal of Bravery, which was only awarded to one other non-Italian — Hans-Joachim Marseille. The "Hunter of Malta" was laid in his final resting place in the soldiers' cemetery of Les Nassen outside of Tunis.

Africa - Sacrifice of the Transport Pilots

Following the successful operations of the airborne troops during the occupation of Norway, the taking of the "impregnable" Belgian fortress of Eben Emael in hand-to-hand fighting, and the subjugation of Holland in May 1940, the campaign in North Africa provided these transports with an entirely new and difficult mission. Despite their operational readiness and willingness to sacrifice, the transports were not able to fulfill this mission in the long run, given their circumstances.

As Rommel and his Afrikakorps began their first offensive on 31 March 1941, the Luftwaffe was required to transport a portion of the supplies from the European continent to Africa. This responsibility was initially assumed by the III/KG zbV. 1 operating out of Sicily. By and by the effort was joined by the other Gruppen of this Geschwader as well as other units. In spite of the high losses suffered by the transports during the Crete operations, during which approximately 150 Ju 52/3m were lost, they were at least partially able to meet the demands placed upon them in 1941. The Gruppen and Staffeln also flew into Africa from Greece and Crete, sometimes continuing on from African airfields with supplies of every kind for the advancing troops.

The Ju 52s flew at low level — often down to 50 meters —during the dangerous crossing of the Mediterranean. At first, their practice of flying in a close formation of approximately 25 aircraft each gave them enough combined firepower to prevent the British from attacking in large numbers. In addition, the formations were usually escorted by Bf 110 Zerstörer aircraft, not to mention the fact that the enemy was kept busy enough defending Malta and his own convoys.

If the losses were kept with in acceptable limits in 1941, the years 1941 and 1942 saw them rise considerably to almost unmanageable proportions, even more so since the resupply of numerous pockets on the Eastern Front (such as Demyansk and Stalingrad) could only be sustained by air transport. Now the transport pilots in the Mediterranean and Africa began to take major losses; the "Massacre of the Ju 52s" on 12 May 1942, roughly 150km off the coast of Derna, serves to illustrate the plight of nearly every mission. On that day Beaufighters and Kittyhawks of the RAF's 250 Sqn. shot down 10 of 13 Ju 52s, fully loaded with troops. Only 47 men were rescued from the sea. A Ju 52 flown by *Feldwebel* Günther Frenzel came down approximately 50 meters from the hospital in Derna. Frenzel, who had four fingers on his right hand shot off, was brought directly into the hospital. On 23 December 1942, he became one of the few transport pilots to be awarded the Knight's Cross for his many supply flights.

After El Alamein was lost at the end of August 1942, the air superiority of the British and Americans became so great that it was nearly impossible to get any supplies at all to the Afrika Armee by air. Nevertheless, the Ju 52s continued to fly, suffering enormous losses. During the battle for North Africa, the sacrifice of these brave transport pilots reached both its high point and its endpoint in the supply operations into Tunisia. The Ju 52s and the Me 323 "Gigant" (Giant) heavy-lift transporters hardly stood a chance anymore, in spite of the fact that they often flew in formations of up to a hundred aircraft under an umbrella of fighter escort. In addition, there were the constant bomber and fighter-bomber attacks which took their toll in lives and airplanes. Nevertheless, they continued to fly up until the bitter end; on 3 May 1942, for example, they were still able to supply the "Tunisian Bridgehead" with 40 tons of ammunition, 68 tons of fuel and 3.5 tons of equipment.

Words and pictures can hardly reflect what the unsung transport crews and the ground crews exhibited in the form of bravery, dedication to duty, willingness to sacrifice and camaraderie. Every single one of them, as well as their good old "Tante Ju" transports, remain unforgotten in the hearts of the African fighters and can rightfully assume an honorable place in the history of the War and the Luftwaffe.

The Me 323 "Gigant" heavy-lift transporter was always a focus of interest. With a wingspan of 55m and a length of 28.15m, coupled with its six 990hp engines, the aircraft justifiably carried the name of "Giant." It had a load capacity of 22 tons, which was the equivalent of 130 fully outfitted soldiers, a Panzer IV tank, or an 88mm anti-aircraft gun. Truly a feat of gigantic proportions! The upper picture shows an E-series Me 323, which carried a pivoting MG 131 gun turret in each wing as additional protection.

As a rule, the Giants flew in groups with as little separation between aircraft as possible, thus increasing their defensive strength against Allied fighters. The photo shows three aircraft flying at low level over the sea toward Tunisia.

An Me 323 ready for takeoff on a Tunisian runway. A Ju 87 about to land can be seen in the background.

The nose doors of this "Gigant" are opened and give an idea of the immense capacity of this monster's "stomach." At the time, the Me 323 had the largest cargo bay of any transport aircraft.

Various types of maritime aircraft were also employed in the Mediterranean region, along the coast of North Africa and in Tunisia. Their use included: reconnaissance, weather observation, anti-submarine strikes, minelaying, monitoring ships, coastal protection, transport and courier flights as well as air-sea rescue operations. The crew mastered these tasks with finesse and bravado. The upper picture shows an Ar 196 (D1+PK) of Seeaufklärungsgruppe 126. Below is a photo of a BV 222 V-1 (X4+AH) of Lufttransportstaffel See 222.

The sacrifice of the transport pilots gradually draws to a close during the Battle of Tunisia and Africa. Yet the dutiful crews of the Ju 52 transports continue to fly into the ever-shrinking Tunisian Bridgehead for as long as humanly possible. ***Above:*** aircraft of TG 1 during a short mission break. ***Middle:*** a Ju 52/3 of III/KG zbV 1 races along the coastline at low level. ***Below:*** a bomb exploded only a few meters from the rudder of this Ju 52/3m of TG 1, putting yet another aircraft out of action.

No matter how desperate the situation becomes, the pilots still cling to their customs and traditions! The beaming *Feldwebel* Helmut Zittler (left) of 7/ZG 26 is seen on his appropriately decorated Bf 110 after returning from his 200th combat sortie.

The tactical recon pilots of 4/(H) AufklGr. 12 also had reason to be happy. The Staffel's pilots and ground crew celebrate the 3000th mission of the Staffel, flown by *Fahnenjunker-Ofw.* Friedrich Stannek (6th from left). Stannek was awarded the Knight's Cross on 12 November 1943 for his outstanding performance on over 400 missions. On 25 October 1944, Stannek failed to return from a combat sortie.

Several tried and tested Jagdgruppen were deployed to the Bridgehead in order to beef up the fighter pilot strength in Tunisia. The men standing in front of the command post of II/JG 53 "Pik As" are, from left to right: *Hptm.* Michalski, *Hptm.* Krauss, *Oblt.* Spettler, *Lt.* Kunz, *Ofw.* Litjens.

***Above left*:** **II/JG 2 "Richthofen" also fought in the airspace above Tunisia. The highly decorated Experten of the Gruppe are seen sitting around a table. From left: *Lt.* Bühligen, *Stabsarzt* (Staff Doctor) Krauss, *Oblt.* Dickfeld, *Lt.* Rudorffer.**

***Right*:** **"Sword Bearer" (translator's note: one who has been awarded the Swords to the Knight's Cross) *Major* Heinz Bär (nicknamed "Pritzl") of JG 77, flew in the skies over North Africa's desert and Tunisia, where he brought down 45 enemy aircraft. (By the end of the war his tally stood at 220!)**

***Below left*:**
Another great fighter ace from Germany who fought in the skies above Tunisia was *Lt.* Ernst-Wilhelm Reinert (second from right) of 4/JG 77. From January until May 1943 he shot down 51 Allied aircraft in the theater, making him the most successful fighter pilot on this front.

Although the Allies commanded the air over Tunisia, the Me 323 "Gigant" heavy transporters continued making their way across the sea, bringing supplies to the hard pressed members of the Heer and the Luftwaffe.

Indian and British prisoners of war were carried back on the return flights along with wounded Germans and Italians. Here a group of prisoners stares in awe at the mammoth-sized aircraft.

By and by, the airfields were lost and immediately occupied by the enemy. A Hurricane IIc of 80 Squadron is seen landing in this photo.

A destroyed Bf 109 G-1/trop (notice the rare triple triangle markings of the Gruppenkommandeur on the fuselage) at the edge of an airfield provides the foreground for an RAF Curtiss Kittyhawk which has just landed.

As an *Oberst* Josef "Beppo" Schmid led a Kampfgruppe from 25 February until the end of March 1943. As a *Generalmajor*, he led the "Hermann Göring" Division in Tunisia until May of 1943. On 23 May 1943, he was awarded the Knight's Cross for his leadership and the brave performance of his soldiers. The photo shows "Beppo" Schmid (right) during an operational briefing with the Commander-in-Chief of the 5th Panzerarmee, *General der Pz. Tr.* Gustav von Vaerst.

Below left:
Shoulder to shoulder with their comrades in the army, the AAA crews, paratroopers and men of the "Hermann Göring" Division fought bravely until the bitter capitulation on 12 May 1943. After heavy fighting, two friends are reunited after having caught sight of each other during a break in the march. Once again, they've survived to live another day.

The "Hermann Göring" Panzer-Regiment also put up stiff resistance. Members of the regiment pose for a photographer during a break along a narrow mountain road. Notice that the Panzer IV is missing its rear left bogie.

One of these brave soldiers of the "HG" Division was *Ofw.* Heinrich Schäfer, who had already been decorated for action on Crete and in Russia. During the final phase of fighting around Tunis, Schäfer's platoon from 4 / JG "HG" held Hill 107 west of Tunis with a strength of only 48 men. This hill was calls the "Cactus Farm" due to the many clumps of cactus plants covering its terrain. Schäfer and his men defended the hill against the most punishing day and night attacks of the British from 28 April until 2400hrs on 30 April, when they were ordered to pull back in the direction of Tunis. Their stiff resistance enabled a new line of defense to be formed just outside of Tunis. The enemy's efforts to take the hill cost 37 tanks and 800 dead and wounded. Schäfer was recommended for the Knight's Cross, which he was awarded on 8 August 1944. The presentation of this award to Schäfer (who was captured on 12 May 1943) took place in mid-August 1944 in the POW Camp Harne in Texas; he was given the medal by an American colonel in front of the entire complement of the camp — all in their parade uniforms! An act of great fairness from a former enemy.

To the victor goes the spoils. Members of 3 Squadron RAAF examine a captured Bf 109 G at the El Djem airfield in Tunisia.

The time draws close for the departure from Africa. Consternation can be seen on the faces of the men gathered in front of the tent of JG 53's commander in La Sebala II. In the center is the commander, Freiherr von Maltzahn, and on his right is *Hptm.* Prinz von Hessen (killed when his plane crashed on 17 October 1943).

This scene took place at the beginning of May 1943, in La Sebala II; members of JG 53 destroy the Geschwader's documents which could not be permitted to fall into the hands of the enemy yet could no longer be airlifted out of the country.

The last remaining ground personnel of Jagdgeschwader 53 enjoy a lunch prior to their journey to Korbous on the Tunisian Cap Bon peninsula. From there it's back to Sicily.

From the edge of the Korbous airfield a few of the best known German fighter pilots watch their comrades make the dangerous takeoffs in overloaded aircraft. The faces of these men register keen interest along with a certain amount of skepticism. From left to right: Schäfer, Lützow, Ubben, Steinhof, and unknown.

Hptm. Götz (center) and *Lt.* Ritter (left) of III/JG 53 are picking up the last men in Korbous. Every Bf 109 flying to Comiso carries an extra man with it. In order to facilitate this, the armor plating is removed and a larger hole is cut into the tiny baggage compartment behind the pilot's head. The "passenger" hung halfway out over the pilot, while his legs went back into the compartment.

Members of the army were not the only ones left behind. The hard lot of a POW — often for many years — also awaited those of the Luftwaffe who served as AAA crews, paratroopers, and members of the "HG" Division. The upper picture shows a collection point shortly before the capitulation. *Middle:* British soldiers offer cigarettes to the men of the "HG" Division after their capture. *Below:* the march into captivity begins for the soldiers of the "HG." For them, the way home is still uncertain.

The graves of many thousands of soldiers who gave their lives during the battle for the "Tunisian Bridgehead" remain behind. 8503 soldiers of the Heeresgruppe Afrika who fell in Tunisia were initially buried in six provisional military cemeteries. Among the fallen were 322 members of the Jäger-Regiment "HG" (formerly FJR 5/Koch), buried in the La Mornaghia cemetery. The shattered remains of a German tank was placed in front of this graveyard as a memorial for all who perished. The deceased Tunisian fighters were disinterred in 1977 and now rest together in the military cemetery of Bordj Cedria.

Aside from the dead and missing, the wrecks of German and Italian aircraft also remain behind, strewn about the now-lost airfields and deserts of Africa.

The orders, honors, medals and certificates survived the African campaign, which has now become a part of history.

The Italian Supreme Command of the Forces in North Africa commissioned this medal in remembrance of the Italian-German campaign in North Africa. It was also awarded to the German members of the Afrikakorps, including those of the Luftwaffe and Kriegsmarine who fought in Africa. The left picture shows the front of the medal, the right picture the medal's reverse. The ribbon is comprised of the Italian and German colors.

Besitzurkunde

Ich verleihe dem

Feldwebel

Helmut Zittier

das

Ärmelband

„Afrika"

Hauptquartier des O. B. S., den 1.5.1943

Der Oberbefehlshaber Süd

Keßelring

Generalfeldmarschall

F.d.R.:

Major

Certificate of ownership for the African armband, which was authorized by the Commander-in-Chief of the Wehrmacht on 15 January 1943 as a "combat badge having the characteristics of a badge of honor." As such, the armband could be awarded to all members of the Deutsches Afrikakorps (Heer, Kriegsmarine, and Luftwaffe) who fulfilled certain conditions (e.g. a minimum of six months of operations on the front).

The many dead an missing soldiers and friends who gave their lives in the Mediterranean and in North Africa remain unforgotten.

High above the Mediterranean, on Hill 87, 6,020 of the 18,594 fallen members of the Deutsches Afrikakorps found their last resting place in the Tobruk Memorial in Libya. Among them, in the sealed underground crypt, is Hans-Joachim Marseille — the "Hunter of Africa."

The Monument to the Fallen Soldiers in Tobruk (above, a view of the exterior) with its memorial courtyard and centerpiece (picture on following page) was built during two years of laborious work and dedicated by the Volksbund Deutsche Kriegsgräberfürsorge. The construction site was graciously donated by the government of Libya at no cost.

On 20 November 1955, the memorial site was solemnly dedicated and a plaque was embedded in the cornerstone which carried the following words:

"This German memorial towers high above sea and desert. May all those who approach it remember with reverence and sorrow these Dead, who, bound by the strict laws of Duty, sacrificed their lives on foreign soil. At the same time, may they also be inspired with a will to devote their entire strength in ensuring that the spirit of Reconciliation and Understanding grows among all People. For us and the following generations, this structure is a Memorial of Peace.

Tobruk, 20 November 1955"

Afterword

As the reader will have noticed, Luftwaffe units have been referred to in the text using their original German terms. The basic unit in the *Jagdwaffe* was the *Rotte,* consisting of a wing leader and his wingman. A formation of three aircraft, called a *Kette,* was also flown quite often. Two *Rotten* comprised a *Schwarm,* and approximately three *Schwärme* made up a *Staffel* (for a rough total ranging from nine to sixteen aircraft). Three or four *Staffeln* formed a *Gruppe,* and three or four *Gruppen* together with a headquarters unit (*Stab*) made up a *Geschwader.* A *Geschwader,* therefore, could conceivably embrace anywhere from just over 80 aircraft to nearly 200 aircraft. A unit's strength also depended on the time period in question; as the war in North Africa (and elsewhere) progressed, the number of aircraft in many a unit would often dropped considerably, sometimes taking weeks or even months to be brought back up to strength. By the end of the campaign, many units were operating with only a handful of operationally capable aircraft. In the text, *Staffeln* are indicated by Arabic numerals, subordinated to their corresponding *Geschwader,* e.g. 7/ZG 26. *Gruppen* are likewise subordinated to their *Geschwader,* but are indicated by Roman numerals, such as III/ZG 26. The reason *Staffeln* are subordinated to *Geschwader* instead of to their *Gruppen* is a logical one: the *Staffel* number indicates to which *Gruppe* it is subordinate. 1, 2, and 3 *Staffel* are subordinate to I *Gruppe,* 4, 5, and 6 *Staffel* to II *Gruppe,* 7, 8, and 9 *Staffel* to III *Gruppe,* and 10, 11, and 12 *Staffel* to IV *Gruppe.* Thus, 7/ZG 26 would indicate 7 *Staffel,* III *Gruppe, Zerstörergeschwader* 26.

An explanation of the Luftwaffe unit abbreviations used in this book follows:

Abbreviation	**Explanation**
(See) AufklGr	(See) Aufklärungsgruppe, or (Marine) Reconnaissance Gruppe
(H)	(Heer), or unit subordinated to Army
(F)	(Fern), or long range reconnaissance unit
JG	Jagdgeschwader, or Fighter Geschwader
KG	Kampfgeschwader, or Bomber Geschwader
KG zbV	Kampfgeschwader zur Versorgung, or Combat Transport Geschwader
Kü.Fl.Gr	Küstenfliegergruppe, or Coastal Patrol Gruppe
LG	Lehrgeschwader, or Operational Training Geschwader
NJG	Nachtjagdgeschwader, or Night Fighter Geschwader
(Pz)	(Panzer), or counter-armor unit
SchG	Schlachtgeschwader, or Attack Geschwader
StG	Sturzkampfgeschwader, or Stuka Geschwader
TG	Transportgeschwader, or Transport Geschwader
ZG	Zerstörergeschwader, or Bf 110(Destroyer) Geschwader

Individual ranks have also been left untranslated and abbreviated as they appeared in the original German text. The following is a listing of the German Luftwaffe ranks and their abbreviations used in this book, in order of precedence:

Generalfeldmarschall	Gfm.
Generaloberst	Gen.Oberst
General der Flieger	Gen. d. Fl.
Generalleutnant	Gen.Lt.
Generalmajor	Gen.Maj.
Oberst	Oberst
Oberstleutnant	Oberstlt.
Major	Maj.
Hauptmann	Hptm.
Oberleutnant	Oblt.
Leutnant	Lt.
Unteroffizier	Uffz.
Gefreiter	Gefr.

Oberfeldwebel	Ofw.
Feldwebel	Feldw.
Oberfähnrich	Ofhr.

In many cases throughout the text, the German terms "Kommodore", "Kommandeur", and "Kapitän" were translated into the English as simply "commander." All three of these titles refer to the commanding officer of a unit (i.e. "Geschwaderkommodore", "Gruppenkommandeur" and "Staffelkapitän") and not to the individual's rank. Generally, a *Kommodore* held the rank of *Major* to *Generalmajor,* a *Kommandeur* was a *Hauptmann to Oberstleutnant,* and a *Kapitän* that of either an *Oberleutnant* or a *Hauptmann.*

Many of the soldiers mentioned in the pages of this book have been noted as receiving the *Ritterkreuz,* or Knight's Cross. It was the highest honor a German officer could receive during World War II, and was actually an extension of another famous German award — *Das Eiserne Kreuz,* or the Iron Cross. It is therefore sometimes mentioned as the Knight's Cross of the Iron Cross and was only awarded to those who had previously received the Iron Cross. In addition to the Knight's Cross itself, an officer could be awarded additional devices to the award: Oak Leaves to the Knight's Cross (Eichenlaub), Swords to the Knight's Cross (Schwerter), and the highest, Diamonds to the Knight's Cross (Brillanten).

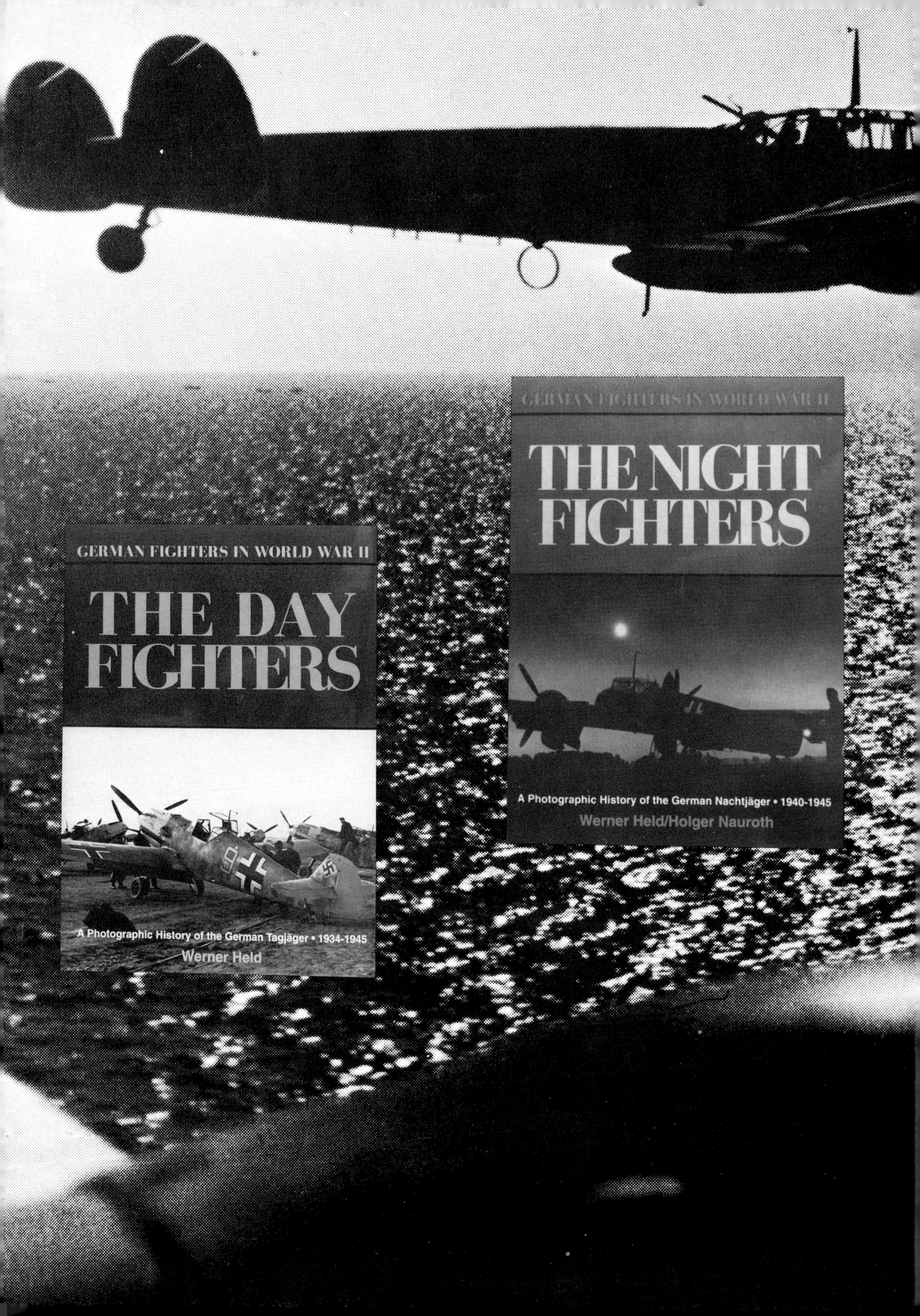
GERMAN FIGHTERS IN WORLD WAR II
THE DAY FIGHTERS
A Photographic History of the German Tagjäger • 1934-1945
Werner Held
GERMAN FIGHTERS IN WORLD WAR II
THE NIGHT FIGHTERS
A Photographic History of the German Nachtjäger • 1940-1945
Werner Held/Holger Nauroth

Holger Nauroth
THE LUFTWAFFE
FROM THE NORTH CAPE TO TOBRUK • 1939-1945
SIX MONTHS TO OBLIVION
The Defeat of the Luftwaffe Fighter Force Over the Western Front 1944/1945
Werner Girbig

MESSERSCHMITT
Bf 109
1936-1945
Heinz J. Nowarra
The Bf 109 F trop of Hans Joachim Marseille of JG 27 (above) and the Bf 109 F of Adolf Galland of JG 26 (foreground).

THE FOCKE-WULF Fw 190
Fighters • Bombers • Ground Attack Aircraft
Heinz J. Nowarra

Ju 88
OVER ALL FRONTS
Joachim Stein

HEINKEL He 100
World Record and Propaganda Aircraft
Hans-Peter Dabrowski

GERMAN GLIDERS
IN WORLD WAR II
DFS 230 • DFS 331 • Go 242 • Go 345 • Ka 430 • Me 321 • Ju 322
Heinz J. Nowarra

He 111
OVER ALL FRONTS
Franz Kober